Letters of Empowerment
to the Next Generation of Men & Fathers

A Reflective Epistolary

Comprised by
Twyla Lee, Ed. S

Edited by
Stephanie Taylor and Twyla Lee

Special Contributions by Everyday Hero's

Men.   **Mentoring.**   **Men.**

SPECIAL ACKNOWLEDGEMENT

Expression of love and thanks go out to God, the Universe and everyone who brought me and the contributors together. This book is the second edition of Bridge the Gap 314 Letters of Empowerment Series. Thanks a Million to the Men who wrote a letter, who unselfishly shared a piece of themselves to make this book a reality.

Thanks Infinity **x** Infinity to our Father, the Universe and to everyone who is a supporter of Bridge the Gap314, Letters of Empowerment to the Next Generation of Women and Mothers book and now Letters of Empowerment to the Next Generation of Men and Fathers book.

With collective effort we all can be "*The White Horse*" that we as a community of people are waiting for.

Tessie Amos III
Cornell Atkins
J. Wesley Bey
LaMarc Bishop
Chad Brown
Mike Boyd
Dr. Ian Buchanan
Alphonso Cotton
Tyrone Davis
Terry Flenory
Dr. Curt Green
Michael Harris
Demarco Jones
Wayne Joyner
Robert Lewis
Alfred Long

Michael McGill
Andre Moore
Tony Morris
Matthew Murphy
Charlton Norah
Ryan O'Neal
Zachery Post
Darryl Reed
Reginald Simmons
Charles Shelton
Jarret Smith
Wesley Taylor
Christian Thompson
David Todd
Nigel Word

DEDICATION

This book is dedicated to the Next Generation of Men and Fathers; Women and Mothers too. This book symbolizes our commitment to building a renewed, united and empowered community.

I love you! I feel overwhelming compelled to begin by saying this. With all my heart I believe without a doubt that Love is the key to keeping each other strong, our communities strong and ready for the world!

At birth or even conception, our purpose in life is assigned to us all. Some of us will realize it, accept it and blossom early on with little to no "Why me" days and then some of us will have so many "Why me" days, times, events, episodes that it's not even a laughing matter. Now, don't jump on the "I know that's the right" bandwagon because I want you to learn to accept the challenge of your "Why Me" Days.

Even though I am a woman and my "Why Me" days probably do not even compare to those of men, I had them, have them…Lucky for me, God equipped me early on with the insight on how to accept the challenge of my "Why Me" days.

Early in my life, I made the decision to exceed all negative expectations that were voiced to me. Now in the process of me conquering challenges, more and more and more challenges came my way. I was literally like Wow! This can't be! But it was and it was! It was because I was *Not* walking in my PURPOSE, I was chasing success and waiting on my day of Redemption from ALL of my Nah Sayers, A.K.A. Haters, you know those who did not do right by me. In other words, I was not being a truly humble person.

I was more concerned with having to prove the point of being right was what was keeping me from moving forward." There is a lesson in every experience we encounter, even if it's a repeated challenge/obstacle. So I challenge you to look at yourself and see what you could have done differently or better.

Take everyone else out of the equation and think selfishly about yourself, what you want out of life, roadblocks/obstacles that seem to be preventing you from excelling to where you want to be. See if you identify common things/themes in your "Why Me" days, times, events, episodes.

In close, the way we think can be the single most detrimental or lifesaving occurrence of our life.

With Love,

From whomever YOU want/need to hear these words from

Contents

Men.   **Mentoring.**   **Men.**

FORWARD

To My Younger Brothers and Future Leaders of the World…

First, I write this letter with unconditional love, for it was with love that our **GOD** created us and what better place to start than from the very beginning, the creation of man. Beloved you are so special that GOD created everything good and perfect for you, before you ever took one breath. Yes everything, from the radiant warm sun, to the bright beautiful moon and stars that light up the night. The soft green grass and every rippling wave in all the oceans were created for **HIS** perfect creation, **YOU**.

HE hand crafted and molded the first man from the brown clay and dust in **HIS** own image. **HE** breathed inspiration into him, giving him life, thoughts and purpose. Life, thoughts and purpose, three simple words maybe not as appealing as fun, riches and fame but they are the greatest gifts the **MASTER CRAFTER** has given you.

The fact that **YOU** were given life is such an amazing gift. It's quite simply your chance to enjoy all of the marvelous creations and sensual stimulation this world **HE** created for **YOU** has to offer. The sound of music, a cool summer breeze, and paintings comprised of many shades of your favorite color or the smell of fresh baked bread; all of these things are processed through your brain, the most superior tool **HE** ever invented.

Our brain is the master key that can unlock any and every door that exists. **GOD** loved **YOU** so much that **HE** gave you a brain that could master and understand everything out here for you to interpret. A brain that is able to comprehend and adapt to whatever it faces. Everyone's brain works in different ways which makes us all unique. Before you were born **GOD** designed your brain specifically for **YOU** because **HE** has a specific purpose for you.

Being a young man, you've probably already asked the questions why am I like this and what am I supposed to do? Especially now when there are so many competing factors and different concepts on what is masculine; how will you become a real man? It can be tough trying to be the man so many others were before you when times are constantly changing. Here's a key, no man is the same even though we all have the same responsibilities. Remember, anyone can do what's "good, **"REAL MEN DO WHATS RIGHT"**. Doing what is right means you stay spiritually focused. Every choice you make is a building block to becoming the future teacher, provider, protector, motivator, adviser and holder of authority you were destined to become. Real men are loyal, faithful, compassionated, inspirational, and committed to standing up for justice. Real men honor their families and encourage others. There really isn't a set age for becoming a man but once the role is accepted it should last as long as you do. A man plants seeds and nourishes the generations of young men under him.

If you are giving it your best effort at all times, you are well on you way to becoming a real man. *NEVER* give up on life. Always strive for greatness and *NEVER STOP LEARNING*. So many times you've heard the names Medgar Evars and Malcolm X. You have probably said to yourself if I could dream as big as Dr. Martin Luther King Jr. or if only I was as brilliant as Dr. Charles Drew. If I was only as bold as Phillip Randolph or had the charisma like President Barak Obama then I could be one of the greatest men to walk this earth. The truth is, no matter how hard you try the one thing you can't do is be somebody else. The reason why is simple, *GOD* has a special purpose for *YOU*. *YOU* are the only one who can be the best you that this world needs!

Time waits for no man, every second counts. Starting now, commit to being a real man, the best *YOU*. The one this world needs.

Love and Peace,
Alfred T. Long Jr.

P.S. "listen *to Imagine by* Kirk Franklin"

INTRODUCTION

We are one and the same…

I received a letter from an incarcerated mother. Her story touched my heart because her story and my story are so very much similar. Just like her I went to college and received a degree, just like her I was a classroom teacher, just like her I have one son, just like her son's father went to prison so did my son's father. Just alike the both of our income was above the bracket for any type of assistance, but at the same time our income was great enough to cover all of our needs.

Unlike her I did not get charged and sentenced for drug conspiracy, but like her I dated the same type of men she did. So it's unconceivable to me that my sister who I have never met or seen has been sentenced to 30 years in prison for a non-violent/victimless crime; for a crime of intent that our government calls conspiracy! It is 2015 and my sister has spent the past 8 years behind bars; in which the last 8 years of my life could have very well been behind bars as well and the life her 18 years old son is experiencing could very well be the life my 16 year old son is living.

We are all uniquely unique, but at the same time we are so similar. We can learn a lot from each other, we can help each other and we need to help each other. All of us were put on this earth to be of service to each other. With this being said if it was me behind bars, my son too would be living in this world without the close presence of his mother and his father just like my sister from another son.

We have to stop separating ourselves from other people's story because their story could very well be our story and what if it was? Wouldn't you want someone to advocate for you, and look out for your child? This book is a call of action to **Conquer Recidivism** and if you want to join this movement send us an email to bridgethegap314@gmail.com and visit bridgethegap314.org to learn how?

With Love
Twyla Lee

P.S. We are all a conqueror over something. Go listen to the words in the song **Conqueror** by Jussie Smollett Feat. Estelle!

PONDER ON THIS...

"Every morning in Africa, a Gazelle wakes up;
It knows it must outrun the fastest Lion or it will be killed.
Every morning in Africa, a Lion wakes up;
It knows it must run faster than the slowest Gazelle;
or it will starve.
It doesn't matter whether you're the Lion or a Gazelle-
when the sun comes up, you'd better be running."

— Christopher McDougall, *Born to Run: A Hidden Tribe, Superathletes, and the Greatest Race the World Has Never Seen*

LETTER ONE

Hello Christian!

I would like a few words with you before you follow the footsteps of the young black men that made the mistake of taking shortcuts in life to obtain wealth. First of all, let me introduce myself to you. I am you, 20 years from now. I advise you to listen. I have some very good advice for you.

I know the flesh is a hard temptation to ignore. Wanting things can make decisions and choices we make very cloudy. Women, clothes, cars are looking so great to you. Acquiring things may seem pretty easy, just by making the choice of selling drugs. But sir this also opens a door that is very hard to close. Do you realize what comes with this territory? Not only direct effects but indirect one's as well.

First of all there is well over a 90% chance that you will get caught and face some sort of confinement. After being caught and no real punishment is handed down, you start to believe that this is fairly simple. Soon it becomes a way of life and what started off as a "hustle" now is a job. If you were looking for a job in the classifieds and the header said get paid large amounts of cash every day. You would be looking for the contact info ASAP. But if you read further and it said you could be killed, robbed, sent to jail or someone in your family could be hurt. I'm sure you would not fill out that application. Well that is what is in store for you if you decide to enter that lifestyle.

There are no shortcuts in life. Anything quickly obtained is usually quickly lost. Mainly because you have no value in it; you didn't work hard for it. Work hard for something and fail at it. Then do it again. When you do reach the thresholds of success I guarantee you feel much better about it. The funny thing is you can apply this to all walks of life.

When I say all walks of life, I am also referring to the women you choose to invest in. Yes, I know they look, smell and feel so great; but trust me you only need one. Christian when you find that one special woman work hard to obtain her love and trust, work even harder to maintain it. But recognize the true ones. Don't waste your physical, mental and emotional attributes on anyone that isn't willing to do the same for you.

So, here you have a cheat sheet for success. You are a very intelligent young man. It will work wonders for you to use the advices I have given you. Now if I know you, I'm sure I do. You won't listen to any of these things I have given you. So here is something you really need to understand. If you decide to pick up that sack anyway! **SAVE THE MONEY!** Chris if you decide to jump up and down on every woman that looks at you twice. **USE RUBBERS!**

Not using the precautions will lead you to being a middle aged man with bad credit and multiple kids by different mothers looking for a new lease on life already behind the 8 ball.

I love you take care of us Peace!

Christian

P.S. listen to *Sky is the Limit*, Biggie featuring 112 Life After Death

REFLECTION PAGE

"It is never too late to be what you might have been." – George Eliot

LETTER TWO

Dear Al,

This is me the future Big Al! I know this is a surprise to you but this has helped us now in the future. This is some friendly advice that you always ignore all the time. It is a song that comes on the radio name the "Greatest Love of All" by George Benson. Please listen to the lyrics on the song. It says, "Everybody searching for a hero, people need someone to look up to. I never found anyone who fulfill my needs, a lonely place to be so I learned to depend on me." This song is our life theme.

Our destiny is in our own hands which mean we must learning to do things for ourselves and not depend on others. When the teachers are teaching listen and learn because you are going to need it for us in the future. One other piece of advice, Do what you have to do so you can do the things you want to do later. Remember when you ask mom can you go outside and she says, "Did you do your chores?" And you did them! We were able to go outside and play! That is doing what you have to do so you can do what you want to do later!

Sincerely,

Big Al the future!

P.S. Live your Life and make me Proud!

REFLECTION PAGE

"A man does what he must -- in spite of personal consequences, in spite of obstacles and dangers, and pressures -- and that is the basis of all human morality." –JFK

LETTER THREE

A Message to the Brothers that want to make a Difference!

I was born on the West Side of St. Louis to a 19 year old lady who already had two kids. Without support from our father, our mother had to raise three babies on her own. She made ends meet I suppose, the best she could with help from family. This was the 70's, so I'm guessing things were a lot simpler in those days. By the time I was six, we moved in with my grandmother and my uncle treated me like his son. He took me everywhere with him until people started calling me his Jr., He was the closest thing I had to a father. My uncle was in the streets and he never attempted to hide if from me. I wanted to be just like him. A year later he was arrested and went off for 16 years, and the only man I knew as a father was gone. It didn't really matter too much because none of the kids in the neighborhood, as well as my cousins, had fathers either, so I figured that this was the natural order of things.

Shortly after my uncle's incarceration, my biological father started coming around. He would stop by and let my sister, brother and I sit in his van while he sat and talked to my mother. Then he would give us a quarter and tell us he would back to see us again. We never went anywhere, but I cherished those visits more than I could ever explain. By my pre-teens I had learned a lot about my father, good and bad. I learned that he helped run his family business which was an Auto Body Shop and Painting (this gave me the desire to do the same thing). I also learned that when I needed him for something I could not depend on him. I can't count the number of time that he told me he was going to do something, only to be let down. But, regardless of what he did, I still loved him and he could do no wrong in my eyes. I always figured it had to be a good reason for him not being able to come through for me. I just never got the answer.

By my early teen years things were changing fast. The crack epidemic had hit urban communities hard and materialism (financial status) was how you were being judged, and nobody wanted to be left behind. Every kid on my block jumped head first into the game. Now around this time is when my father gave me the worst advice ever in my life. Trying to keep up with everyone else, I leaned on my father for money. That's when he told me that I lived on a block where drugs were being sold and that I should try to get paid too. He told me that I could be good at it because I'm a street dude and he knew I was not soft. So that became my hustle and I must say my Pops was right cause I did OK for myself. I was able to help my mother out, as well as my siblings.

In 1996, I was arrested on drug charges and was sent to prison. I reached out to my father, only to be given the cold shoulder. He told my mother that I was on my own cause I got myself into that situation. I was devastated! How could a man who encouraged me to do something, who had done it himself, turn his back on me in my darkest hour. It was then that I learned that my father had never sold drugs, or even broken the law. That was the first time I realized that my father did not care about me at all. He only wanted to keep me outta his pockets. I was no longer going to make excuses for his short comings.

Armed with this new hurt and pain, I vowed to never let my kids go through or be treated like they are not loved or that I do not care about them. Once released from prison, not only did I stay true to my word, I volunteered at the community center and started coaching young boys in sports. I tried to show my children and others that through discipline and hard work anything is possible. I want my children to know that I care about them, and I want them to care about themselves. I believe every young man needs a strong, positive man in their life, and it doesn't necessarily have to come from the home or from your father. I have no ill will towards my father because believe it or not, he made me the man I am today. His actions as a man made me a better man, from all the hurt came love for my younger brothers, and I can thank him for that.

Peace,

J. Wesley Bey

REFLECTION PAGE

"Men are like steel. When they lose their temper, they lose their worth."

Chuck Norris

LETTER FOUR

Marc,

I hope this letter finds you in perfect health and spirits because I'm about to tell you some things that will definitely shape and help you on this road called life.

As a little boy you need to listen to your mother. Understand that she's doing the best she can at raising you. I know that you wanna be around your dad but know that your mom has your best interests. She's not perfect but she's perfectly made to raise you. Know that she's not the enemy and her rules are made to protect you and not humiliate you. You have to stop lying and sneaking. It's only going to make things worse. Everything that you think you must tell a lie about to get immediately; you can get the same thing later by honest means. This will teach patience. Your mom is trying to teach you discipline. Without it you'll become a statistic. So know that your mother will give you everything that you'll need to survive in this world...

It's also very important for you to get a good education. Yes, I know that school isn't your thing; in fact, you're not very good at it. But you need to apply yourself and do your absolute best. If your best isn't good enough, then do even more. Because you will need more than a high school diploma. Education is priceless...

As a little boy I do not want you to be afraid to tell if someone is making you feel uncomfortable. Know that it is not ok for your mother's girlfriend to kiss you in your mouth like you're grown. It does not matter what she says, it is not alright.

Now as you get a lil older you're gonna want to do what you see your friends doing. But be your own person. Don't be a follower. ...be an individual. Don't worry about who's having sex. Girls will be around till the end of time. Don't be in a rush because you'll wind up in something you're not ready for.

Now when you become a young man you're gonna meet a woman. Terri is her name. First of all, **_DO NOT_** have sex with Terri. She will cause you more stress, shame, embarrassment, tears, guilt and rage that you will ever experience. I'm asking you to handle her differently. Unfortunately you can't avoid her because eventually she's gonna give you a lil girl, your daughter Brianna. Brianna will be the most precious creature you have and will ever see. But with Terri you need to practice patients. ..She can learn from you. Show her a different kind of relationship than what she's used too. Every opportunity you get, reason with her. Understand that she is a product of her environment. Because I know this woman is going to put you through pure hell. This is where discipline comes in. Terri is going to try to keep your child away from you. She's going to lie on you. She's going to say you did things that could put you in prison for a long time. So use wisdom when you deal with her. I definitely don't want you to go through what I went through. But then again on the other hand it did make me stronger. It made me see and realize that *I CAN NOT BE BROKEN*

One of the main reasons, I'm still solid is because I love myself. You need to love who you are too. On those days when nothing seem to matter, including your life, look around you and see how many lives you affect; cousins, aunts, your brothers. You matter to so many people around you. Without self-love you'll start seeking attention of woman all walks of life. You'll wind up marring somebody who you're not in love with. Someone who you don't deserve to call a wife and someone who doesn't deserve to call you a husband.

The Bible says, "He that finds a wife finds a good thing". Marriage doesn't come with instructions but here are the best tips.... Be in love, selfless, willing, mature, stable, prepared, generous, and be honest. When you make a covenant with God, you promise to love honor and obey for richer or poor through sickness and through health. ....these vows are serious. These vows make a covenant with God that you don't want to break. Now I'm not saying you can't get it back but why even risk it?

You need to tell your first wife that you're not in love with her. Do not disrespect your marriage by bringing other woman into the home you and your wife live in. If you continue that kind of blatant disrespect, you will develop a bad sense of entitlement. You'll act as if rules don't apply to you. You'll become reckless and consequences will be the furthest thing from your mind. And if you continue that behavior you'll find yourself in a place where no man wants to be...The Department of Corrections, the Big House, The Joint, The Slammer, or just Prison. ...Every man's nightmare.

That's why it's important for you to make choices that will help your life and not hurt it. Man get your shit together now!!! You can't afford to waste any time. Be productive in a positive way with everything that you do.

Develop personal relationships with God. Let Him lead you and order your steps. Learn to trust Him and let Him have His way in your life. Understand that your life has a purpose and a reason.

Humble yourself and when necessary be truthful with yourself first. Remember this if you lie to yourself, lying to others will become extremely easy. But you will **NEVER** progress in life on lies. I hope you understand all that you've read. Use it and keep it close to your heart.

Take care...

Marc

P.S. "**You Gotta Believe**"! Listen to *When You Believe* by Mariah Carey and Whitney Houston

REFLECTION PAGE

"After a certain age every man is responsible for his face" - Albert Camus

LETTER FIVE

"A Strong individual takes the bricks that are thrown at him and uses them
to build a solid foundation"

- Unknown Author

I guess it's safe to assume you're a few steps ahead of the rest… The fact
that you're reading this implies you possess initiative. Curious, the last
decision you made, was it your own or was it influenced by
Pressure…Emotion…Fear… Haste… Were you riding the wave of
unconscious to project a certain image or was it thought out clearly? Surely
you know that seeds planted will eventually bear fruit of some kind… I ask
because so many have fallen prostrate to the idea of economic advantage or
the acquisition of wealth by any means necessary being the answer to all
situations. At what cost? Societies view of what is or isn't, what should or
shouldn't, has caused may to form alliance of some sort with moral-less
values that they allow to define them. The effect, they're willing to
sacrifice whatever's required of self to gain an unrealistic end. I say
unrealistic because most are living for the moment, so as long as things are
(mis)perceived "Halal", they deem their situation "Kosher". As for those
that settle in this life style as if it's a career – "Insta-Gram", this message is
from Club Fed compliments of the mandatory minimum career offender
401-K Plan set up by the government. Hey! They use to do 100 to 1, how
about them odds. Imagine that, from strip mall and clubs to disrespectful
overseers, controlled movements, long lines (No V. I. P.), bunk beds,
shared showers, and depending on where you are housed- restrooms reek
of piss, how's that for bliss…

-IJS

I know who I – Right… I am one of the many whom no matter the
demographic – share a similar reality. Right now we've aligned for a
common cause;

-You…

I represent those who we have forgotten; I've had the privilege of
navigating the very cloud you're riding. I'm the faceless voice via written
expression, reaching out to "the me" in you… This message is an attempt
to get you to take a moment to reflect, see past the obvious. I spend so
much of my time replaying any situation over in my mind – looking at it
from different scenarios thinking if I'd done this instead of that…
overlooking the true cause… "Self…" We are the choice we make. I know,
I know, you're good… You're with a thick tight clique, mob, family, etc…

Those around you quote: "I'll go to the grave before I become ah b- - - h figgah, but when the Feds come callin', they answer low pitch snitch n - - - ahs". Your reality in that game, everyone you are true to isn't necessarily true to you.

-Respectfully…

What is it that I want or expect from you? I expect you to use the same initiative that has you still reading to make a difference. Find your purpose, fix your aim. My future is unclear yet I'm optimistic because I now know my past doesn't define me. The choices I make now will shape who I become. It's sad that motivation is contagious… we're wired to mimic what we see.

"A world is supported by four things: the Learning of the Wise, the Justice of the Great, the Prayers of the Righteous, the Valor of the Brave…"

-Dune

"Which are you"?

"Your indecision to make a decision is in fact your decision to accept things as they are…"

-Author Unknown

Siddiq

REFLECTION PAGE

"Big jobs usually go to the men who prove their ability to outgrow small ones." -   Theodore Roosevelt

LETTER SIX

Chad was it worth it?

As a kid growing up in the late 70's and 80's, I fell in love with football from watching my older nephew and his friend's play. Around the age of six, I got my chance to play with them, even though they wouldn't tackle me that hard to find out that I had speed, moves, toughness, and the "IQ" that it took to play the game. My nephew David compared me to a small Tony Dorsett, a running back for the Dallas Cowboys during that time. That's when I was put into the Junior Football League and started my dream of becoming the best football player ever. I played all the way through High School and had many offers from every college in the nation. I even went on several college visits so I could decide which one I wanted to committee too, but then certain things started to happen.

As a younger teenager who was on top because of my athletic skills, girls started to notice me from being one of the top guy's in the school. That was a problem because it started to cloud my mind on school and sports but I was strong enough to overcome that and maintain. But also during this time of my life, drugs were introduced to a lot of guys that I was hanging around with. I was wasn't interested in drugs at that time, but seeing that most of my friends had money in their pockets and buying what they wanted, and I couldn't, had me curious. So, I tested the water's but instead of me just getting the sack from the neighborhood supplier I would just call one of my friends over when I knew someone that wanted some work. That way I wouldn't have to hold anything from fear of my mother or worst, the Police!

During this time I lost my nephew David to an asthma attack and my Step-Father to pneumonia, they both died. The next three back-to-back deaths became my breaking point for me to cross over to the "*Under World*" as I would call it; and probably changed my life forever was when I lost my Mother to Cancer, Biological Father and my Grandmother back to back. I *Did Not Know* what to do! Football was out of the question… it was the last thing on my mind at that time. My mind was so clouded and with no father figure or mother I turned to my friends and started doing what they were already doing, which was selling drugs…

As the years passed and I learned the laws of the streets, I ended up passing most of my friends up in this new life that I inherited. I graduated from a low level to a level so high up on the drug chart that it wasn't no turning back. I was supplying half the city with this new money maker. I ended up expanding to multiple cities after linking up with these two brothers from Detroit that I met from one my Homies out of my city. I had many mansions in several cities, all the cars you can think of from, Bentley's to Lambo's, the finest jewelry, and the finest, foreign women, that we called "*Foreign Objects*"! (Lol) I met and partied with all of the celebrities, you name it I did it… In 2002, I had my little girl and my life was set! Who wouldn't want what I had accomplished? Mansions, money, a family, and trips everywhere, I was on top of the world!!!

"**BUT**", and there is always a "**BUT**" in everything that you do and say and like I said, "**BUT**" then everything started to crumble like the Twin Towers…

Indictments started coming down around 2005 for our crew. They started coming from several cities and them people (the FEDS) was swooping in grabbing everybody and everything they could. The money, the cars, the houses, and the women, all was gone. The friends that you thought you had…Gone!!!

Your family members, who were jealous of you because you wouldn't do what they wanted you to do for them, went and took what they could from your spots that the feds didn't take! Half the crew told on us because they couldn't do the time... This is the same crew that we bought everything for. If we road exotic cars, they did too.

It was every Man and Women for themselves; I stood tall and ended up with 16 years on my first offense. I have been watching my daughter grow up in here. It's all fun and games until reality sets in when the agents come knocking at your door. Now, I don't have a place to call home anymore all because I put the game and my friends before my family. I have to eat out of trays that everybody eats out of. I'm not sure who washed the trays I eat off of or even if the tray is clean. I am told when to wake up every morning and move when these people tell me to move. I have to share eight bathroom stalls with 200 inmates in one unit. In here I have to share eight urinals with these 200 inmates. In here my fellow inmates and I have to deal with all of the staff members attitudes each and every day. Please know that if one inmate messes up, we all get punished for it. I sit back and think about my life and I keep asking myself each and every day, "*Was it Worth It?*"

I wrote this letter to you, my younger me so that you can see that trying to get things the illegal way isn't the best way... There's an old saying that I use to hear back in my day and I still here it today "*All money ain't good money*" and that's the **TRUTH**! Do the right things gentlemen. Follow your dreams as a young man. You'll change your mind many times but change it for a better, positive way. It's no fun over here where I'm at. Stay out in the world by getting what you want accomplish the long hard way...

I pray that by you reading my life story that you'll get the right message... May "God" bless you and watch over you... FOREVER!

Love Always,

"Chad J-Bo Brown"

P.S. listen to 'One Sweet Day (with Boyz Ii Men)' by Mariah Carey.

REFLECTION PAGE

"Few men have virtue to withstand the highest bidder."

George Washington

LETTER SEVEN

Dear Youngster *Game is Like a Piece of Fame…*

It is no accident that I was approached to write a piece about my life. I've always had visions that I would write about myself. Now that this challenge has confronted me the certainty of it has given me mixed emotions. I am afraid and conflicted about what to share. I know in any event I must be honest. It is hard finding the beginning of my story, so much has happened in my life, as I try to unravel it all and put things in order to help me understand how I arrived to where I currently am took a great amount of discipline and time. So as I look back in chronological order I remember being on a cliff, looking down thinking that if I fall how far would I fall to my death, then I remembered that I made a conscious choice that this is where I want to be. Today I am 58 years old and I'm still paying for my choice of pursuing "*Game Fame*".

I think first I should share with you where I come from, which will give you an idea of why I chose and did the things that I did. I was born in Pruitt-IGOE. My mother and father had 13 kids. I was the 8th child born. I believe what makes my life unique to me is that I did not know that we were "*poor*" living in Pruitt-IGOE. The **PROJECTS** is where the poor lived.

At an early age, I knew that I had leadership skills. Having the ability to think for others had its advantages and disadvantages. I started stealing when I was 7 or 8 years old and during this time, my life began to change. My life quickly changed because of the interest I had and the interest that others took into me.

My older brothers interest in me, began one day when he called for me to come into the bathroom with him. Once I was in the bathroom with him I was amazed at what he wanted with me. My big brother asked me to simply hold his arm and to squeeze it as hard as I could. Of course I was confused; I had no idea what he was up to, but I did what he asked of me. As I was standing in the bathroom I watched my brother began to ramble through a pouch. While standing there I noticed an eyedropper with a needle and at that very moment, the realization of the moment intrigued me and as things began to unfold I became even more intrigued. My brother had some capsules which he emptied into a wine top and from there he stuck the needle into his arm and told me to squeeze his arm *HARDER* and from there "Sweet Dreams"...

This is how I entered into a world unknown to anything I've ever imagined. This was my first experience, my first dose of heroin. Until this day, 51 years later is how long I've been dealing with this drug. Nothing in one's childhood can compare. Being that I was so young and inexperienced, I did not realize that I was entering into a world and mingling with a group of people that had its own rules that were all so very dangerous. If you weren't a fast learner you could be dead and it wasn't because of the lack of knowledge that could kill you at times.

If I could tell you exactly what intrigued me or kept me in this lifestyle this long it would be that the "*Devil's*" offers were too damn good to turn down. Honestly, this troubling lifestyle swallowed me up and still has a hold on me. I thought of nothing beyond what had just happened to me could ever be more exciting than what I had just witnessed. And the sad part is that I did not try to think beyond it either.

It is so many ways to get trapped. I cannot begin to share with you how or which one caught me up. I was told later, that the life, the feeling that I chose "is nothing but illusions; **NONE** of it is real"... But the death I narrowly escaped from, that haunts is very real to me. I've lost so many friends and there is nothing ghostly about that. My friends are dead and nothing is going to bring them back. Once you realize that and you let it sink in you begin to understand *CHANGE* is only possible if YOU want it and begin to work slowly for the change you want.

My bird's eye view has so much blinded hindsight that I struggle to maintain the honesty my story deserves. I struggle because if I really share all that I am feeling and all that I have experienced such as the freedom, the curiosity, the fun, the carefreeness, and the lack of consideration I enjoyed as a youth I could go on for pages and pages. I also struggle because I find it hard to find words to convey my current wisdom because what I witness, lived and enjoyed as a kid, I know that I should not have.

The weight of my youth experiences and the way that I enjoyed living is different and the same for youth of today. The weight of **PROJECT** life is unique and different from HOOD life because living and loving your environment is just as detrimental now as it was back in the 60's. When I was growing up they sang "We Shall Overcome" and today youth chant "Fuck the Police", "Hands Up, Don't Shoot", I Can't Breathe, Black Lies Matter" etc… and I wonder did my privileged curiosity of the underworld give birth to generations of hurt and neglected youth of today? Did my chase of *"Game Fame"* contribute to the twisted lifestyle that youth of today eagerly sing lyrics of how things are? Did my blindness to politics a contribution to the hurt and frustrations of youth today? My mind races…

My environment and the people I grew up around made me grow up fast too. But as I examine what was within me, I realized how my life was different from other kids and adults. Some adults back then just as adults now would be in *"total shock"* to know what my friends and I aspired to do, to be like and what my friends and I plotted to see. The transformation of truth is difficult for some, but the transparent sharing of truth is a way to correct the ills of choices not well thought out.

Let me be clear about what I'm sharing about my life. What I saw, heard, participated and things that shaped my mind, thoughts, opinions, and future are all of a *twisted* good. I use the word *twisted* because my path to now was not straight even when I thought it was. The depth of what I felt and aspired to be as a kid has to be conveyed carefully because in **NO WAY** do I want to come across as if I am aspiring one of you to live the way that I choose to live. What I want to convey is *"the environment that we grow up in does not have to define who we are, or our choices"*. What we choose to allow excite us is how we end up living a life that we never would have imagined or dream of.

My intro to my story may bore you as it would bore some of my friends. My stories of someone getting killed or O'd-ing on dope in my building would bore some of them because they had seen the same things just as some of you have. Now when I told people who did not live in Pruitt IGOE what I had seen or did they would be absolutely glued to my conversation "shocked" and afraid for me. They would look at me with wonder as to why my parents allowed me and my sibling to live in such an environment.

They also wonder why I sounded so excited telling my childhood stories. It's simple; the truth is, I lived a double life.

I was the son of a Strong Black Woman and the son of Proud Black Man. My family life was nothing like my outside life, my parents weren't aware of my outside aspirations, just like parents of today. Why didn't my parents know? They did not know because deception was a part of my "Game". Nothing was more captivating to me than the "*Game*" even at 7 or 8 years old "*I Loved the Game*". I loved going outside getting with my friends, going stealing from store to store and knowing that everyone had an item to steal. You see I was the leader of my crew, which gave me added "*Purpose*" and it also gave me more certainty as to why I should not aspire to do anything else. My environment and my thinking totally ruined the innocence I had in me. The reality of daily life in the **PROJECTS** created a whole new life in me and in my friends. My friends and I would watch the guys who had dope, who they gave dope to, even where they would hide their dope and yes my crew and I would steal the Dope Man's Dope! When we stole the Dope Mans dope all chaos would come.

Sometimes guys would get pistol whipped or even killed and knowing the possibilities of what could happen did not provoke any sadness in my friends or me, we hustled harder. We stole the Dope Man's dope on plenty of occasions. It became our business; this was the way that we made a living. We would get up early in the morning on pursuit to know what we needed to know to do our job.

The summer of 1967, my friends and I witnessed more murders than trees we climbed. Earl Jr. was the guy that was doing most of the killing he had graduated from shooting people in the leg and started killing guys who owed him money. Again this fascinated me, I was witnessing something no other kid would ever see or could stomach. Even with these realities of growing up in the 60's; in this era was the "*Best*". I thought my life was perfect and all of my friends who lived in the **PROJECTS** with me thought the same thing. The only damper in my life as a youth was in the Summer time when my parents sent me to the country. I would hate being in the country even though I would have fun, I hated being away from the Pruitt-IGOE. I would Daydream about what was going on in the PROJECTS. This is crazy, I know now but it was the way I liked to live because it was fast paced, an experience that some kids could never imagine. Game is like a piece of Fame and in Pruitt-IGOE I was Famous. Imitation is the purest form of flattery until you're on the other end of Dope!

In closing, Am I my Brother's Keeper? Youngsters don't make choices that keep you in captivity.

Love,
Unk
A.K.A. Wes

P.S. Go listen to Marvin Gaye *What's Going On*

REFLECTION PAGE

"It is not titles that make men illustrious, but men who make titles illustrious."   - Machiavelli

LETTER EIGHT

To My Mighty, Mighty Men of the Future,

My name is Tea Mack and for the last sixteen years, I've lived my life from inside of a Federal Prison. Nevertheless, I believe that it was written that I experience this path in order to establish the necessary credibility that I may be qualified to instruct and guide a particular warrior class of young men spread all across the world.

And my message to you all is as follows:
I don't think that there could ever truly be enough said to stress the importance of the company we keep. As these 16 years of my life began to fall like grains of sand inside an hour-glass. I found myself always thinking about all of those male and females whom I'd spent so much time with. It was then that I began to realize how very little I really knew about most of them. The little information I did know made me lean more towards terminating, rather than maintaining friendships with these individuals and yet they managed to remain within striking distance.

Of course my first reaction to this reality was an emotional one, I immediately proceeded to label what I was experiencing as an act of unfaithfulness and betrayal. But as the years continued to fall, I slowly but surely came to the full realization that these relationships only existed as they applied to me because I gave them my permission.

It was my shallow thinking that blinded me to the long-term effect and significance of having qualified people around me to support me on all my righteous endeavors. I also grew to realize that with the right people around me, anything that I dreamed of accomplishing was possible. But with the wrong people, everything that I dreamed of accomplishing would be in jeopardy.

The future is yours,

-Tea Mack

P. S. "Thinking is the very essence of and the most difficult thing to do in,business and in life. Empire builders spend hour after hour on mental work…While others party. If you're not consciously aware of putting forth the effort to exert self-guided integrated thinking… Then you're giving into laziness and no longer control your life."

-David Allen

REFLECTION PAGE

"When men speak ill of thee, live so as nobody may believe them." – Plato

LETTER NINE

Dear Brother, Brodie, Homeboy, Young Man, My Younger Self,

I pray that the Supreme Powers of the Universe that you are alive, well, vibrant and productive as well as proactive. I've kept my ear to the street in order to maintain the 411 on your progress, growth and nurturing. It's a shame that your decision-making has been manipulated, guided and twisted by the inhuman demons that forced us to take 10 years for one STONE!

I pray that you choose to play ball in another arena because, as you can see, the streets is the fast track to death or the joint! Providing for your family, education of self and the world around you is true empowerment, not quick fast CASH and ASS. You know exactly what I mean.

From our bumpy road, I must say that the most important thing I; We have learned is to NEVER give up, BE happy and allow our good character to shine through all adversities so that when we look at ourselves in the mirror, we will Love what we see.

With Love and Hope,

MDJ

Dear Younger Me,

My advice to my younger self would be to discover my purpose and passion in life EARLY! Be committed to development, and nurture MY OWN DREAMS.....Understand that the Journey comes in small steps.....Finally Believe that God is directing my every step!

Believe in Yourself,
D. Todd

REFLECTION PAGE

"There is one kind of robber whom the law does not strike at, and who steals what is most precious to men: time." - Napoleon

LETTER TEN

To the Youth of the Present:

Even though this letter was written at some point in time; you are reading it now. There are many way to go with this and all of the thoughts can become a novel in itself. I will try to touch on a few key points.

We all start life at the same point but progress in different stages. You are given those points when they are supposed to BE. You only get one time to do things first. First words, first steps, first time to fall in love and so on. The rest are chasing emotional responses to try and relive that first.

There are two ways we go about life. We learn what to do and what not to do. The people, influences and environment play a part in the way we go about those things. Our parents tell us what not to do, but a lot of times don't tell us why not to do it. When we ask why they see it as a challenge. The end result is "because I said so." What household is not affected by drugs in some way? A lot can be avoided by learning WHY? Just because things are new to you does not mean there is no one close to you who can tell you the end results. Growing up I've seen things from the street corner crack and heroin sellers, the users and the million dollar dealers. I looked at how people with good jobs and things went from maintaining to homeless. They used to rent their cars to 14, 15, 16 year old kids just for a high. Not thinking about how they were going to get to work tomorrow. The lucky ones got their cars back. The others got them out the pound or never got them back because they were wrecked. Thousands of dollars of consequences for a $20 piece of crack. Some did get upset, so they got another piece and they were cool.

Being in this environment makes you guilty by association and then peer pressure will eventually catch up to you. It all starts off with drinking then smoking weed. You are lucky to stop there. That is where a strong peer group comes into play. Over time some will stray and curiosity will grab hold to a few. The main people who sell drugs often end up using some type of hardcore drugs. A few people who sold crack ended up using heroin and some even smoking themselves. Those people you see standing at the liquor store or walking the streets ended up in a predicament that they are in as a direct result of them being about that life they couldn't shake loose.

A lot of people will start selling and everyone has their own reason whether it's because of the lack of having necessities. Parent(s) doing all they can just to get you clothes. When you get to school and around your peers you get clowned because you don't have J's or you wearing store brand clothes. You think you have to impress that girl you like. You want a car. If you don't tune that out you will fall into the trap. Those things will come to you in time. A lot of times BETTER. I looked at small people catch drug cases one by one everybody started going to jail. It's something to listen to in a black community. Yea, such and such just got home or went away. Listen in the white community, same sentences but different places. Jail in the Hood and College in the Suburbs. Once I saw a real moneymaker go away I said it's not worth it. You can have a good 2 to 5 years of rolling if you are lucky. Also, if you are lucky you get to go to jail for 10 years. Your kids grow up, you miss their lives. Technology passes you by. The world changes and remains the same altogether. The unlucky die…bottom line. You are on a hot ladder people who don't know you will set you out to dry. You won't figure out "Who's Snitchin?" or is setting you up to be killed.

The things that come with living the life… It's all **FAKE**!

You stack the deck against yourself. The cars with rims bring attention such as tickets, police harassment, getting jacked or your car being stolen altogether. Then you see your rims on a car just like yours. So now you got to get'em back and gunplay comes into the picture. I remember in 98 when 20 inch rims first came out. Some guys jacked a dude and killed him while his daughter was in the car. Now the rims are factory on a lot of cars today. Dude lost his life, daughter lost a father, all for some rubber and metal. Would a person kill for rubber bands and spoons? The same material just comes out of a different factory. It's worthless. It all becomes worthless as time goes by.

The best thing you can do with drugs is to **JUST SAY NO!**

You don't have to be first to do things. You don't have to do some things at all. Look at the first ones to have sex. I remember in junior high school. There was a girl who just had a baby. She was 14 or so. Everybody treating her as if she was special... That's not special. Her mother has to raise another baby because she was a baby herself. At 3 pm I'm going home to play video games, hang out or whatever I was doing. She had to go home and change diapers and make bottles. Think about it. How much can you actually teach a baby at 14 years old. You read the baby books and can barely read yourself. THINK!!

There were others talking about going to the clinic, getting shots and pills for STDs. That's not cool. Learn and act responsibly. Get yourself established first. We have a higher percentage of people who will have children first and then try to deal with establishing a foundation. We must first establish the foundation and then start a family. Learn to establish credit, buy a house, car, furniture and then start a family. Try to think a minimum of five years ahead. Don't think about the hood because as time progresses you will mature. The hood mentality should no longer work for you. We are where we are because of what we did in the past. So YOU! Must do POSITVE things in your present!

In closing, my name is not important but my message and love for you the next generation is as real.

Sincerely,

X

P.S. "The only Black person who drives a Phantom in the City of St. Louis owns a funeral home. **WAKE UP!**" Go listen to WAKE UP EVERYBODY - (Teddy Pendergrass, Harold Melvin & the Blue Notes)

REFLECTION PAGE

"An eye for eye only ends up making the whole world blind."
– M.K. Gandhi

LETTER ELEVEN

Dear Young Man,

I have been given the most wonderful gift ever. I have been granted the opportunity to talk to you from the year 2014. I know it is 1980 where you are. I also know that you are in the middle of your first year in high school. But hopefully this miracle of an opportunity will allow me to impart some useful words of wisdom to you.

First of all, always know that you have the capabilities to do whatever you set your mind to doing. I know that is a cliché, but it is true. Now everything will not come easy. Some things will require you to work harder than you ever have, but it is possible. Figure out where you want to be and work out a plan on how to get there. Post that plan on your wall so that you will see it every day. Let it be your reminder to do something that will move you closer to your goal. But, also know that like time changes, so will you and your goals. That's ok! If you see that your goals need to be change, then change them. You are the master of your destiny.

Secondly, please understand there is no shame in failure. You will fail... LOTS OF TIMES perhaps; failing at something is not a bad thing. Sometimes we need to fail until we learn to get it right. The inventor, Thomas Edison, tried out hundreds of different material to perfect the incandescent light bulb before he found the right material. He didn't see the previous attempts as failures, but as steps to the solutions. I know the word failure will cause you to hurt and because of this you will not want to try. But you must not give into that negativity. Just understand that failure is a part of success.

As you grow, many people will cross your path. A lot of these people, whether they are family, friends, teachers or even strangers will share their wisdom, like what I am doing, with you. Listen to them. You may think you know everything, but you do not. You have only lived a fraction of your life. There is no way you could know everything. No one could. But these people will enrich and enhance your life. You do not know it yet, but they will help shape and guide you. Think of them as Angels sent by God.

Now you are always free to disregard their advice, but before you do, always listen to what is being said and ask if there any truth to what they are saying. You will know if the message strikes a cord within you.

While people can be useful in guiding you, do not let them define you. You are a unique individual created by God. I know you are wondering "who am I?" You are struggling to find your identity. Being African-American is tough. Society has one view of who you are. Your family has another view. But who are you really? That is the question only you can answer. Shakespeare once wrote in Hamlet, "To thine own self be true". Heed this advice. You are on the road to discovery. Embrace the journey. I am telling you it is alright to be studious even if your friends may not think so. Learn to be comfortable with who you are. Never be afraid to let the real you…"*the you*" that live deep inside…the you that you long to be …never be afraid to become what you really are.

Finally, remember the fact that many people have given much in order for you to have what you have today. They have sacrificed much; some have even given their lives. You must pay it forward. Share your experiences, both good and bad, with someone who needs to hear it. Shed the mantra of "*Me First*". It isn't always just about you. In your life as a teacher, (yes you will become a teacher) you will run across many students who have the same doubts, the same fears, and the same issues you are going through now. When possible listen to them and share your experiences. Perhaps that is why God allowed these experiences to come to you, so you can be a guide to someone else. Be a part of your community. Become active and knowledgeable in civic life. Do not let other people take your choice away. You have power, exercise it.

I wish I could tell you more about the future. You have a great future in front of you. Always believe that you are worth being loved and have much love to give. The road will not always be easy but use every difficult obstacle along the journey as fuel to reach your final destination. A lot of people you know will start this journey with you but they will not be with you when you reach the end. Do what you can to help them in their journey and you will find in the end you have also helped yourself. Your future is waiting only for you to shape it.

Take care always and keep the faith!

Charlton Norah (2014)

P.S. When time permits listen to *"You'll Never Walk Alone* written by Rodgers & Hammerstein from the musical Carousel (1945) Alicia Keys version

REFLECTION PAGE

"We can't change the world unless we change ourselves."

-Biggie

LETTER TWELVE

Dear Self,

You are going to see, hear, and feel things growing up as a Black Man that's going to make it hard to not lose control and get angry. Protect yourself, your women, and your people. Keep moving forward through all of the non-sense. Make your parents, your family, and your friends proud.

If I could go back to our adolescence, growing up as a Black Man in this world, I would tell you:

1. You are a strong Black Man!
2. Dictate your value and worth. Always hold your head high.
3. Decide your core values and never waiver from what you believe.
4. Be a leader, proud and strong.
5. Make your own way. No one knows what's better for you than you.
6. Work hard and earn everything that you deserve. Focus
7. Make your own, good, decisions and never look back. You are in control.
8. Show the world your heart and demand respect.

Be proud of being Black but, do not let being Black define you.
The world is a strange and insecure place. The people in it will try to judge you and treat you based on the color of your skin. That is their ignorance, do not acknowledge it. Always rise above the weak mind-sets and fly!

Sincerely,

Me STL Dre

P.S. listen to Big Sean - *One Man Can Change The World* Ft. Kanye West & John Legend (Dark Sky Paradise)

REFLECTION PAGE

"A man is a success if he gets up in the morning and goes to bed at night and in between does what he wants to do." - Bob Dylan

LETTER THIRTEEN

I never understood why my mother was so hard on me as a young man, I was called a nerd because I had to carry myself a certain way. I wasn't allowed to hang with certain people because she didn't approve of how they carried themselves. I use to try and plead their case as if she didn't understand and she was just being mean.

Now, I understand she was preparing me for life and how to see through the games of life, I found out the easy way that everyone is not your friend. The song Back then you didn't want me but now I am hot and you all on me is so true because I love saying that I made it out the hood safely and now I am a productive part of society, I am able to help others and that makes life even sweeter.

I grew up right in the heart of the city and now when I go back to my old schools and see how they have closed down or either they have changed it to an alternative school I just get more focused to make sure I tell my story "**DON'T GIVE UP**". I see that the village once was here is gone and the tough love that was here is gone too.

This new generation has to make a new identity and I want to be a part of it. I learned patience a long time ago and unfortunately this new generation wants everything right now and that just makes life harder because life has changed and normally whatever comes to you fast will probably not last and that is something most people don't understand.

One thing I want to leave with you all is to follow your dreams and don't let anyone hold you back. Take the time now to find out who you are and build off of it. Times have changed so it isn't that easy but I realized that today's generation is built for these current times and that was proven just by being on West Florissant during the protesting.

Tough Love means just because you aren't given all of the nurturing that is often needed to understand how to deal with your conscious. You have to be strong enough to handle the mindset of today's society and prosper even in the midst of your storm. Your storm can come in many forms so keep your eyes wide open because you may lose someone close to you or you may find yourself on the streets and feel abandoned and I see a lot of that because of the field I currently work in. I tell all the young men I work with you are never alone you just have stay focused and believe…..

Charles Shelton

<u>Teens of Tomorrow</u>

REFLECTION PAGE

"The trouble with not having a goal is that you can spend your life running up and down the field and never score." – Bill Copeland

CHAPTER FOURTEEN

Dear Nigel,

I'm writing you this letter from the future, it's 2015. I realize you are living in the year 1980 during a time when you are beginning to learn about the world around you and how to make decisions for yourself. As a student in junior high school, life seems really simple and at most times myopic from your perspective and life experiences.

I can see you sitting in your English class listening to the teacher talk about a very important lesson, which you will need later in life. But, you don't hear a thing coming out of her mouth until you hear the principal's voice come over the PA system. The principal announces that President Reagan has been shot; the class gets emotional with the news being reported about the President. This news has caused mixed feelings in the classroom which you are not able to process what you are feeling; let alone thinking. I've been told President Reagan is the president for the rich not for the poor or working people, which you feel you are a member of the bottom group. You try to make sense of how to feel for someone you feel who has hurt your family in a time when Blacks have to work so hard just to get the basic necessities in life. At this stage in your life, you see the struggles your parents are going through to make life comfortable for you and your sisters, gas prices increasing, and food expenses determining what meals are cooked at home.

Also, you hear the white noise from your parents that you should carry your wallet at all times with your student identification in it. You know you don't understand why this message is being drummed into your consciousness, but you know it's for a reason. Even watching the evening news has subliminally caused you to think differently about where you live when you hear references to North, South or West county/city. You're not fully able to make heads or tails to these labels of the geographic areas of St. Louis, but you know it means something. Then as you grow older, your parents' messages get louder and louder. They tell you not to be in a car full of other guys because the police will definitely pull you over, don't linger too long or pick up anything when in the departments stores unless you are going to buy something. You've got to be twice as smart than a white person in order to make it in this world.

This is a lot to take in all at once as a boy, but you will find your own way through this maze to survive as a Black Man in this society. Nigel, I want you to remember, you determine your destiny in life; I'm not saying you should turn a blind-eye to the circumstances and situations you will experience in this world, but you make your own decisions for your betterment and those around as you evolve through this thing called life.

Love,

Nigel Word

P.S. Go listen to *Break Every Chain* by Tasha Cobbs

REFLECTION PAGE

"That which doesn't kill us makes us stronger." – *Friedrich Nietzsche*

LETTER FIFTEEN

Dear Lil Ryan,

We grew up poor, our parents were on drugs; our mother and father did not provide us any structure at home. We came and went whenever we pleased or wanted as you use to say. Days would pass without us eating. Yes, we had it hard for real. So at the age of 13 we started hustling because we were hungry and to have what all we needed, we understood that we needed to hustle harder and in order to hustle harder the most logical solution was for us to quit school.

We felt like we were a man because we were able to provide for ourselves and for our little sister. The first name brand clothing our sister and us ever wore and had was because hustling. We hustled to provide for ourselves, for our little sister and most of all to have what we did not have. When we were fifteen we got us an apartment and soon after we got our own apartment all the material things began to pour in. Everyone loved us, so we thought.

As I reflect on this point that *"everybody loved us"* is when one has money, or someone can help out. Everyone loves that one person because of the possibility of what that person can do for them, how they can brag on being close to you. **BEWARE IT's NOT REAL!** We know this now because we are in prison and now the one's who had us drunk on the feeling of how they loved us say that we are dumb and they knew we would be sent to prison, they were psychic Lol!

Our time in prison has taught us that NO Matter how long you can get away with selling drugs, if you don't stop its going to catch up to you at one time. Our very first drug charge landed us straight in Federal Prison. We were twenty years old and our mother's sister, yes our aunt told us she had a guy (a plug) that wanted to buy four ounces of crack. Our auntie use drugs, so we told her "ain't no way" but she asked us to do it for her and she pleaed, she said she just wanted to make a few hundred dollars. So, we agreed but told her that we did not want to see the guy at all.

Remember it played out like this, we picked her up walk'n down the streets, she had the money on her and she got into the car with us and we handed her the drugs. A year later the D.E.A kicked my door in, we weren't at home, but our daughter and her mother was there was at the house. Until this day, five years later they still remember how *"them people*" came into our home, pointing guns at them. So yes, I'm arrested, in jail and on a visit my lawyer shows me a video of "the" transaction with our Auntie. She had on a watch with a camera on it. To our surprise, we learned that our auntie set us up to free her son from prison. That literally broke our heart, this lady who we loved, who changed our pampers traded my freedom for her sons; my cousins… We couldn't eat for days, we were sick.

Ain't no love in them streets! The streets ain't for no Good Dude at all. No matter how bad your situation is, the streets ain't a option, the streets are for animals guys who lack morals, respect for themselves or others. The street life will either murder you or send you directly to prison. Life is full circle the life that I thought I was hustling away from landed us in basically the same conditions that we were fleeing. Lil Ryan having to constantly looking over your shoulder watching for the cops and the robbers ain't worth the hype. Lil Ryan remember you are putting your whole family at risk. The moral to this letter is that a lot of times dudes like us get in the streets so young we don't know what we are signing up for. Yes, we hear about this person went to prison, this person got killed but we still go chasing down the same road like we know something that others did not know.

In the end the streets ain't gone get you on nothing but a T- shirt that say R.I.P or Free whomever…if that is what you want a short life and a few dollars then I guess the streets and prison are for you.

Love,

Big Ryan

P.S. Listen to Lil Boosie- *Moma Wonder Why Your Child So Bad* this helps me understand the ills of society that we all must learn to combat in a positive way.

REFLECTION PAGE

"I don't care whether you're driving a hybrid or an SUV. If you're headed for a cliff, you have to change direction". - Barack Obama

LETTER SIXTEEN

This is from OG Wayne, to Young Wayne.

Listen to your Mother, because all our mother's ever wanted for us to be was a respectable person in life. Rarely, do we ever pause and think about all the pain our mother's went through to bring us into this world.

Just stop and think for a moment, without listening to your Mother.

If you are looking up to people with these types of names, Rolls Royce Ronnie, Maserati Rick, Water Head Bo, Freeway Rick, Icy Rivers, it just a matter of time before you self-destruct, because they are into the life, where there is no love in the streets… You never want to wait till your mother has passed away before you can say these words, BE Man Enough to say them now! *Momma I Love You!* I never want to hurt you, cause you any type of distress, nor embarrass you.

They always say, if you know better, you would do better, and now that I know better, I'm going to do better Mom. I know all you ever wanted for me to do is get an education and be somebody. The life I chose, and the path I took, not only caused me heartache and pain. I know it cause you heart ache and pain as well, and my kids too. But Mom knows the life I choose today, I believe you would be proud of me, because now I strive and believe it's about doing the right thing. The life I choose now is about freedom, and not behind some Damn Prison Walls. I just hope and pray that you will look down upon me, and see that me, your son is now doing the right thing, so you can R.I.P.

To whoever reads this letter, if you have never listened to anybody before in your life, do yourself a favor, the biggest favor you could ever do for yourself… Hear Me Now, I've had everything a man could have ever dreamed of in this life, I'm talking about the best of the best, I was part of a $270 Million Dollar Operation, which some, if not most of you, probably have heard of called (BMF), Black Mafia Family.

If you don't listen to me just keep doing what you doing, and I'll see at one these counts that happen at 4:00 pm, 9:15 pm, midnight, 3:00am in the morning, 5:00 am, and at 10:00 am on the weekends, and you'll get the chance to meet me and some of my friends in person if you keep doing what you are doing.

Maybe me and my friends are some that you might look up too, but

KNOW that I'm the one who was blamed for giving BMF the Drugs, and having the connections and now this acquisition has landed me a whole lot of time in the FCI, I guess my connections weren't good enough.

For those of you who are listening to your mother or to whomever is raising you, tell her that you love you her; say Momma I love you, and let her know that the man you are becoming, is all because of her, and say I thank you for giving me life.

Your's Truly,

Wayne (AKA Big Weezy).

P.S. *"*Listen New Edition's *Boys to Men*

REFLECTION PAGE

"The only thing worse than a man you can't control is a man you can."

– Margo Kaufman

LETTER SEVENTEEN

Bri...

How are you? My hope is that you're doing well...I often find myself thinking about you. Sometimes more than I'd like too. See...the fact is that I feel like as a father I failed you, it haunts me. I feel like it's my fault you didn't finish school and had a child at a young age. It's my fault that you didn't turn out successful as we both dreamed instead of being a statistic. I live with this certain guilt.

When I found out you weren't my biological child I was crushed. How does a man, erase 7 years of joy from his heart and mind? How does a man forget about birthdays, preschool, doctor visits, quiet times, moments in the park, potty training, pictures, silly moments and being called daddy?

I hated your mother for many years... I hated her for manipulating me and brainwashing you. I hated her because she took my dream and turned it into a nightmare. She stole my happiness and turned it into anger and rage, she made me dark. Please know that because GOD has forgiven me...that I have now forgiven her. And if you have hatred me/her in your heart I pray that you too forgive us.

I want you to know that having you in my life was so much of a joy and the memories of the joy still bring a funny kind of joy and achievement. You made me believe that I could accomplish anything. To hear your little voice say "good morning daddy" was music to my ears... The day I found out you were not my biological child, my heart was shattered into tiny little pieces. I became a bitter man, I wanted to hurt someone else because I was hurting, I was hurting so bad Bri! Still today, I'm still trying to get over the hurt you not being my child caused me. I cry, when I see father's and daughters together. I cry when I see the way my brother's daughter look at him. Emotions a gambit of emotions because I recognize that my brother is his daughters hero and that she is his masterpiece, then the memories of you and how you made me feel pour over me.

Brianna I dreamed of giving you all the wisdom and knowledge I have...I wanted to see you in your prom dress, teach you how to drive, help you get your driver license, clap for you as you received your high school diploma and college degrees. I envisioned walking you down the isle on your wedding day, kiss your forehead the and give you to your husband and to let your husband know that you are LOVED! I wanted you to speak for me at my retirement ceremony. So many dreams I had and of my dreams imagining your future was shattered by one huge lie!

But today I only know the seven-year-old little girl you were on a fatal day. I don't know who you are today... It wasn't in God's plan for me to know you today, I wonder why because they say it was for my good; your good but the good hasn't unfolded for me yet.

I often wonder if you think about me the way I think about you. I also wonder deeply what kind of relationship we could have at this stage in our lives. Would you take my advice? Would you listen to what I have to say? I want your life to be as wonderful as you'd like it to be. I pray for your health, wealth and well-being. I pray that God will bless your life now and forever.

I love you!

 Your Dad

P.S. Listen to Whitney Houston *All At Once...* take care.

REFLECTION PAGE

There is no better than adversity. Every defeat, every heartbreak, every loss, contains its own seed, its own lesson on how to improve your performance the next time. - Malcolm X

LETTER EIGHTEEN

Dear Curt Jr. and Jordan,

I am writing you this letter now so hopefully when you're an adult you will reflect on this and it will have some meaning later in your life. I want you both to know that you are two of my most important accomplishments in my life, and seeing each of you grow in your own way each day makes me the proudest dad in the world. At an early age, I realized in order to become the man I was raised be, it would take leadership, scholarship and tenacity. I stayed the course, remained faithful and exceeded all expectations!

As I reflect on my past experiences when I was your age, I didn't have to face the harsh realities that you are experience as you mature into adolescence. In fact, Black boys were not perceived as public enemy number one. Black boys were not poorly educated and dropping out of school at high rates. Black boys were not incarcerated at higher rates as compared to their counter parts for similar offenses. And the police did not see us as violent thugs who should be shot down in the streets, or choked to death while standing at a storefront. No, my sons, it was expected that I graduate high school, and go on to college! It was expected that I make the right decisions for the right reason and at all times. Yes, my sons, I was raised by the "Golden Rule," do unto others, as you would want others to do unto you.

So, as you both self-reflect and become fine young men, I want you always to remember the morals and values you have been taught at home. Be thankful your grandfather instilled in me perseverance, tenacity, and the ability to stay the course. Without him as my role model and providing guidance in my life, your character development wouldn't have been possible. Remember your grandmother who loved you unconditionally regardless of the circumstances and always gave you more than you ever needed. Be mindful it was your mother who was relentless in nurturing you both with prayers, direction, and a strong desire to see you each reach your full academic potential. Remember your big sister as a role model, a voice of wisdom, and how you two can succeed in all that you put your mind to if you live within the guidelines set by your mother and I. Most importantly my sons, never forget the words of your uncle, "always look up to the sky and say a word or two, – Amen x 2".

As I sit here and self-reflect on role as your father, I hope I've lived up to your expectations. I tried to develop you both to become socially emotionally prepared to take on the world. A social emotional developed young man is prepared to succeed in the classroom as well as in life. As a father, I wanted you to be confident in all of your endeavors from your academics to athletics. So I made sure you had *self -awareness.* It makes me proud to know you can stand for what you believe is right and understand that one's actions have consequences in terms of others' feelings.

I know you don't always agree with the decisions of your mother and I, but your ability to *management your feelings and express them constructively is an awesome character trait you both have acquired.* Son your drive and determination to accomplish a goal is like no other I've seen. Don't lose that spirit, to whom much is given, more is expected. *As you cross off items on your bucket list, be mindful to not step on the backs of others – always be willing to show them there is a lot of room at the top for others. Finally son, always surround yourself with like-minded individuals. Your ability to forge lasting relationships will be key on your way to the top.*

To the best sons in the world: Curt Jr, and Jordan, thank you allowing me to be your father. You are destine to be great in life, continue to be the best you can be and always strive for greatness. No matter what challenges you face in the future, know that I am your #1 fan; you can always count on me. As I have said before, I always put your needs above mine, and will drop anything I'm doing in a second if you need me.

Thank you for allowing me to be your father, you have taught me so many things about life and myself in general. I am a better man for having this opportunity. I want to instill in you everything I know, and how to carry on the family name with dignity and respect. One day I will not be on this earth, and you may feel all alone, but I want you to know I am always with you.

I love you, always and forever.

Your Dad,
Curt

REFLECTION PAGE

"One voice can change a room, and if one voice can change a room, then it can change a city, and if it can change a city, it can change a state, and if it change a state, it can change a nation, and if it can change a nation, it can change the world. Your voice can change the world." – Barack Obama

LETTER NINETEEN

Dear *Fatherless Son,*

I'm writing to you on behalf of your father. I know if he were here with us today he would be proud of the young man you are becoming. He would be proud not only because you are a scholar athlete but also because you are an honest, loyal and a stand up type of guy. I can see him smiling on the sideline at your Football Games. I can hear him saying that's my son and I hope that you can too.

Baby Boi, always know your Dad would parent you through your teenage years and talk to you about the dangers of **Blind Loyalty**, and he would stress to you the equal importance of being a good friend and being a good son, grandson and family member. Your dad would instill in you the importance of spending quality time with your family and showing people who you love that you love them. As you all talk, you all would share mannish laughs and swamp stories of good ole times. In the mist of the laughs your Dad would touch upon how fast time fly's when you are having fun.

In the mist of guy talk you would catch some sadness in your Dads eyes and from his eyes you would understand how much he values the time he spends with you. On some occasions he would apologize for missing out on so many of your Milestones and you would know without a doubt that his vows to never miss any more of your Milestones are sincere.
Before me or anyone else could interrupt y'all time, your Dad would hug you, tell you that he loves you and ensure you that he's always going to be with you regardless to whatever.

Your Dad would tell you himself how bad he felt and feels from being away from all of us all the time he was. He would tell you that his time away from his family and us brought the importance of making good decisions to the forefront of his mind. He would explain to you that he accepted the fact the decisions he made led him astray but also brought him to realize what really matters. Your Dad would tell you to never to jeopardize your freedom or to gamble with time. He would tell you that his greatest regret is his lack of good decision making prevented him from being able to show the people he loved how much he loved them and from spending time with those who really matter. I know your dad would say all of these things to you and more because he said them to me when we discussed our aspirations for you. Your dad and I often talked about the type of person we wanted you to be. And I am proud that you're well on your way to being exactly who and what we desire you to be and achieve.

It hurts me that someone "*shot*" your dream of having a father-son relationship with your Dad... like having him at your games, cheering for you on the sideline or in the bleachers. It crushes me that someone gunned down the possibility of you and your Dad having mannish talks and laughs. It kills me that someone killed your Dad's future and his opportunity to spend time with all of his love ones. It angers me that you and so many other young people today, have to grow up without a Father because of senseless gun violence.

In closing son, remember to be loyal to yourself and your family first. Learn to be good with taking the long route because, short cuts lead to set backs and your Dad paid the ultimate price for taking short cuts, blind loyalty and trusting the wrong people. Your Dad thought he would have more time to *"**hit right back**"*… Don't gamble with time son!

Forever with you,
Michael McGill

P.S. *"*Listen *to Song Cry by* Jay-Z*"*

REFLECTION PAGE

"Don't aim for success if you want it, just do what you love and believe in and it will come naturally."   - David Frost

LETTER TWENTY

Dear Self,

In the name of our Lord and Savior Jesus Christ, I salute you. May our Father in heaven bless you with all of the desires of your heart.

I pray that these few words from the heart reach you in the best of health and spirits. I know all of that sounds foreign to you but one day you will be enlightened in the ways of God. One of the most important things I can express to you is to seek a true relationship with God. He is the gateway to all the desires of your heart. He will teach you how to love yourself which will in turn teach you how to love your family, friends and the women that he will choose for you to spend the rest of your life with. As your heart opens up your choices and your decision will never be selfish, but selfless.

Time you have on this earth is precious not one second can you ever get back. Pursue a higher education. It will open many doors for you in the business arena. Never dumb yourself down because of the company you keep. Help them rise to the occasion. You were born to be a leader. Lead from the front; Understand that every decision you make can change a person's life forever. I know that your father wasn't in your life from a young age, but that has given you the strength courage desire and discipline to press forward. Never forget how you felt on so many holidays when your father wasn't there. Remember the conversations you wanted to have but couldn't. I said all of that to say, be that shining light in your kids' lives that your father wasn't to you. Instill in them every drop of knowledge that you have within. Lead by example. This can only be achieved by you being present. Money is no substitute for your presence. What you feel you were missing in your childhood may not necessarily be what they miss. Open up a healthy line of communication with them and truly listen to what they say.

One of the most precious things God put on this earth is a woman, and so she should be treated. Not lied too, cheated on or disrespected. Never pursue a relationship with a woman if you don't plan on giving her your all. She deserves you best and nothing less. Every King deserves a Queen and when you are blessed with your Queen love her with all of your being.

When a man fines a wife, he finds a good thing and obtains favor of the Lord.

Know that you will have highs and lows, trials & tribulations all throughout your life. Embrace, cling to and welcome all those experiences knowing that they will shape you into the man God has destined you to be. Everything you learn in life, you have a duty to pass those experiences & knowledge along to empower the men and women that you come in contact with throughout life. As you set short and long term goals for yourself, know that God will never put anything on your heart and not give you the tools to accomplish them. You are who you say you are and you can become whomever you choose to become, even the President of the United States.

All is well. "By faith"

Love,

Self...

P. S. Listen to *Never* by Scarface and *Nobody Greater* by VaShawn Mitchell

REFLECTION PAGE

"Always be yourself, express yourself, have faith in yourself, do not go out and look for a successful personality and duplicate it."

-Bruce Lee

Letter Twenty-One

Dear Boss,

I was giving the title **BOSS** at the age of 12. As I sit here in my jail cell... I watch every moment pass me by. Year after year as my children graduate from high school, after hearing about every sports event of theirs I missed. I sit and think about how powerful choices are. I missed my children going off to college; I wasn't there when my children had their children. I missed every pivotal point in my children's life and now even my grandchildren... Then I think about how I left the mothers of my two children out there to raise and protect our children by themselves.

Life went so fast for us! I was a child with the responsibility of a grown man. About the time I graduated from high school, I ran the biggest drug dealing enterprise in Oakland Ca. I became very popular with my peers adults and Very, very popular with the women in my community. I was a "**BOSS**" My uncle turned me on to the game at age 12. I started out as his look out guy in 69 Village in Oakland, California. I had a strong sense of leadership that put me on top very fast once my uncle went to jail. See he was my idol a "Drug Dealer" in my neighborhood there was not any Teacher's, Lawyers, Doctors, etc...

Dealers and the Pimps were the people we idolized without knowing the repercussions. We just saw the material things that money could give you like **Power, Respect**, cars, jewelry and women. At a very young age I was exposed to this and that when my appetite grew... I wanted to be a **BOSS** just like my Uncle. Before the age of 20 I had everything. I had Old Schools Cars, a Convertible Corvette, a Benz, a Turbo Porsche; a Brand New Maserati's and front row seats at fights. I popped bottles all the time, all the bottles I could buy... I was a **Millionaire** before I turned **20 years old**. I had **Power** and I had women. But all that I had and was doing was very short lived and ended before I could legally purchase alcohol.

As I speak to the youth in me, that's in you know that there is only 3 things that are guaranteed when you partake in life that I choose, you will possibly face jail time, die young, or you end up using drugs yourself. I lost so many friends to this game. When you sign up for this life it's much harder than it seems. Your responsibility to everyone else becomes much greater and you never make enough money because the weight of the community becomes your problems. Everyone becomes dependent on you for help or to look out for them.

My choices have caused my mother so much hurt. I have cheated myself from a quality life. I caused myself pain and many people have suffered from the bad choices I made for choosing a life that always has a DEAD ending. If I would have took my organization skills as a "Boss" I could very well be a CEO of any major corporation today. I could have the same material things such as a beautiful wife, my children and parents would have not had to pay for my wrong choices. I would not be writing this letter from my jail cell after serving 26 years in prison of my 35 year sentence.

I was arrested 8 days after my 20th Birthday for manufacturing Crack Cocaine in Oakland, CA. I have been in jail since 1988. As I speak to you, the youth in me, let me tell you that this is not the life you want. You now have great examples of what you can be with President Barack Obama and Michelle Obama 1st Lady of the United States, I idolize these two. Don't choose the neighborhood drug dealer like I did. I say find out what type of lifestyle you want to live. See what type of education it will take for you to get to the lifestyle you desire. Keep your credit good and your criminal record clean. Good credit and a clean criminal record is a prescription to becoming a real "*BOSS*" today.

In closing, I would trade every expensive car, every dollar I made, every title I was giving in the streets for the chance to raise my children, to hold my grandchildren and for my mother and sisters not to spend another holiday or shed another tear with me inside these walls. Federal Prisons has become my home for my entire youth and adult life.

Much Love,

Darryl Lamar Reed "Lil D" because **BOSS** got us lost into the U.S. Criminal Justice System

P.S. listen to Jay-z *Fallin*

REFLECTION PAGE

Coming together is a beginning; keeping together is progress; working together is success.

- Henry Ford

LETTER TWENTY-TWO

Hey how are you my younger self?

I know it's been a long time since I tapped into your thoughts. I've learned a lot since the last time we conversed. I was reckless, I admit this young man, putting us in harmful, wreckful situations. If I'd listened to my mom's and granny, I mean we would not have gone through so much turmoil…

I witnessed older Homies get murdered right in front of our face and witnessing death of Homies didn't discourage us from the streets. I actually wanted to be just like the *Big Homies*. Yes, I wanted to have the big cars and a light skinned woman with the big curly hair. Lol!!! I didn't pay attention to the signs of being naive, but I would find out in years to come.

The streets don't love anyone. I wish I would've stayed involved in sports and school. I had to be dumbest person back then! I should've prepared better for your future younger self. Naturally we were born to shine, but I didn't realize or value what God had given us.

Our Father who art in Heaven, gave me life and multiple opportunities to be anything in this world but I chose to sell Dope and Gangbang. I lost majority of my friends… remember all them dudes I use to run with? They are dead or in prison for life... How I look at it now, is that I'm not successful, because I ran from the right knowledge to join the wrong knowledge...

Forever with you,

Self A.K.A. Mike Boyd

P.S. listen to *Dear Mama*, by Tupac shaker R.I.P. this song inspires to do and be a better man

REFLECTION PAGE

"Patience is a virtue, and I'm learning patience. It's a tough lesson.
                                                           -Elon Musk

CHAPTER TWENTY-THREE

We live in a Country where our current President is African American; our current Attorney General is African American Women, one being the most important person in the world and the other to apply the Laws of Authority.

However, we as men of African American descent are being killed at an alarming rate on a daily basis. Another way of getting rid of the African American male is to kill him by putting him on the New Plantation (equal to Mass Incarceration).

My painful experience of being an African American in these great United States of America I do have many wonderful memories; nevertheless, these times are hard to cope with seeing so many young men being gunned down by police officers, Zimmerman and other agencies. As an African American male my advice to young men would be two subjects; one would be to understand the laws and rules of these Great United States, while the other would be for you to study and continue your education until you finish your program of study.

Laws and rules are very important to know because ignorance is no excuse for breaking the law. Lacking knowledge, being untaught or illiterate doesn't mean you won't be held accountable for your actions. To know laws and rules of these great United States gives us as African Americans a level playing field.

By not knowing the laws and rules we fall victim to unfair policing, dirty politics and live our lives below the poverty line.

By understanding tax breaks, voting rights ad democracy we can change our futures from not so bright to very promising.

Learning to be patient through studying has changed the way I use my time. My day starts with physical education, second is the study of HVAC (heating cooling and ventilation), third I'm taking college courses at Coastline Community Jr. College improving body, mind and soul is my overall goal!!

Speaking to you from Federal prison, where I have been living for the last 20 years of a 30 year sentence, I have hope that some of you young black men reading will take some of this message and begin to change your lives.

In closing, be of the thinking class and not of the **DEAD**!! Much love and respect to all the young men who were lost in battle and hope to those of you caught in the struggle.

Sincerely the older you,

Matthew Murphy

P.S. *"Believe in your Brand"*!
                                        -Unknown

REFLECTION PAGE

Stop waiting one other people to give you permission to do what God
already appointed you to do!   -Shanel Cooper Sykes

Chapter Twenty-four

To My Young Soldiers:

As a brother raised up in the tough, character-building community of East St. Louis, Illinois, transitioning to a major Midwest university to pursue an Engineering Degree I did not always see the light at the end of the tunnel. But I persevered to become an educator (and a 21 year-old parent), there are so many life lessons that I could share however, young sir, there are certain things in life you must experience personally in order for you to truly appreciate the lesson.

You can't develop the game it takes to be a leader if you don't go through fires, fuck ups, failures, and falls. If I could share a few keys to crossing over and dunking on the inevitable challenges life will present to you and becoming the hall of famer you were meant to be, I'd suggest that you do four things:

a) have a scary vision

b) surround yourself with inspiring friends

c) work harder than anyone you know; and

d) prioritize joy.

First, you must have a scary vision. That is, the dreams and goals you have for yourself should not be limited by anything. Dream big, dream a little bigger, then dream twice as big is that. If people aren't absolutely amazed (and a little bit skeptical) about your vision for your life, your vision is too small.

Most of us have big dreams…and most of us get off track at times. A key to staying on track is to surround yourself with people who can keep you motivated and inspired. Never forget the saying that "steel sharpens steel." People like Lebron James, Barack and Michelle Obama, and even Jay Z didn't become great by surrounding themselves with underperformers. Lebron skipped college to play in a more competitive environment. Both President and Mrs. Obama went to top universities and Jay Z has learned financial literacy from some of the wealthiest entrepreneurs in the world.

Third, success is about outworking anyone who's in your lane. If you aren't working while others are asleep, don't expect to reach your full potential. It is no accident that Stephen Curry is one of the best pure shooters the basketball world has ever known. The thousands of hours he has poured into his craft is now reaping tremendous benefits. You should literally *"recognize game."*

Lastly, over the long haul, life is more fulfilling if there is joy in it. The profession you commit to should provide you with a sense of joy. Find work that means something to your soul, and find ways to keep your life balanced. Enjoy hobbies and activities that give you joy as well. All work and no play makes us black men with hypertension, high blood pressure and a first class ticket to a premature death.

Have a big vision for your life, surround yourself with motivated people, work harder than anyone in your lane and intentionally enjoy life. See you at the finish line of Success!

Peace,

Ian Buchanan

P.S. listen to *Never Let Me Down* by Jay-Z and Kanye West. "

REFLECTION PAGE

I also believe that you are what you have to defend, and if you're a black man that's always going to be the bar against which you are judged, whether you want to align yourself with those themes or not. You can think of yourself as a colorless person, but nobody else is gonna.
– Don Cheadle

LETTER TWENTY-FIVE

To the Adolescence Tyrone Davis's of this World:

Stay in school, and work hard man. Befriend and surround yourself with the best and brightest students in every class you have. This is something you will have to learn to do, in any endeavor you have throughout your life. Being armed with this knowledge will make a difference in whether you get a passing or failing grade in school.

Don't be afraid to ask for help, and remember, there is no such thing as a stupid question. Besides having a formal education in public school, you are going to also need self-education, and that means reading books to get answers to questions, instead of turning to friends and family first. You may be surprised at how much, or little someone knows about a given topic.

Even though you may not be getting groomed and critiqued for success in the home environment you live in, you have to continue to be self-driven and motivated. Remember, if you don't quit and give up at whatever it is you are striving for to better your life, you can never fail, it just might mean that you have not met a time constraint placed on you, or self-imposed, but you are not a failure.

Learn to listen to your inner voice, especially when it comes to matters of morality, and do unto others as you would want done to yourself. One of the best places to find moral guidance is in the Church, or a Masque. I find the teachings of Jesus and Muhammad to be very sound and practical. Join one of the above houses of worship, and don't just talk the talk, but also walk the walk, and keep it *100* with yourself when you fine that you are doing something that you know Jesus, or Muhammad would not do.

In worldly matters, you're going to have to be more of a leader, than a follower and what I mean by this is, that sometimes you are going to have go out and do some traveling down unbeaten paths alone to get to where you want to be in life, and trust me. There are going to be some painful set-backs, but you know what they say, no pain no gain.

Don't get caught up in the cow herd effect a lot of us fall into, because of something or way of living seems to be popular and cool by many. For instance, a lot of us are living way beyond are our means, and will never be able to save money for a rainy day, or get ahead in life. This is mainly because our values and priorities are out of balance. Instead of spending on practical things, we go out and buy all kinds of fancy name brand cars, clothing, and jewelry trying to keep up with the Jones's, without ever really realizing that we can't really afford them. So what you have to learn to do is dictate on paper what you are going to be doing with your time and money in the near and not too far future, to find balance in life.

Also, we live in a complex world where you got to be aware of your social surroundings politically and now more than ever economically. We as a people have made great strides politically in the last 50 years, but not economically. After achieving political success in the 60's, I think everyone assumed that we all would be fine economically and things would get better. Well I want to let you know that things won't get better until we as a people learn to pool our resources to create our own economic opportunities. Once we as a people take up this responsibility, we will start to see real progress, and start to experience true freedom, justice, and equality in this country. Take advantage of the Internet and Social Media, and patronize Black Businesses for your goods, services, and necessities as much as practical.

Now, that I've talked to you about some of the things that you can change in your life and the lives of others in a positive way, let me talk to you about some of the things that can change your life for the worst. Please stay away from gangs and drugs, and save yourself from a lot of heartache and pain, because jail is no fun place.

I'm-ma be straight up blatant with you and tell you this, the Government and Law Enforcement in this country are disproportionately targeting and locking up young men and women of color men up with draconian (of laws or their application) excessively harsh and severe) sentences that last for decades in an attempt to kill us off. If not stunt our growth and development as a people by legally disenfranchising us after a felony conviction. In the areas of education and work for reasons unrelated to the crimes someone may have committed. The effect of this is a systematic way of controlling us and reducing us down to second-class citizens, just one step above slavery. Now you do the math.

Sincerely,
Tyrone Davis.

P.S. listen to *One Mic* by NAZ; I want you to listen to this song because…

REFLECTION PAGE

"The pride of young men requires that they seem wise, despite their inexperience, and the only way to appear all-knowing without going to the tedium of acquiring knowledge, is to hold all knowledge in weary-seeming contempt." — John C. Wright, *Awake in the Night*

CHAPTER TWENTY-SIX

A Church Boy is what they call me...

As a third generation guitar player, I must admit that I have been blessed with a talent and a powerful relationship with the Lord that has saved me many times. As a young boy and still today I am Blessed. I was able to bond and develop a shared passion not only with my father but my grandfather too this passion provides for me and my family. My father and my grandfather instilled a love for music in me which also introduced me into a market that will not experience any crashes, or send me to the unemployment office and my work place is one of the traditionally safest work places. My employment not only provides a way for me to make a living but it allows me to work doing something that I love and makes me feel as if I'm not working at all. This talent of mine provides steady employment and weekly nourishment and insight for my soul. This talent and my work environment has kept me in times when I was in places and doing things that I know I should not have been doing. For this reason I am always reminded to be thankful for surviving to be able to be a walking testimony of faith.

My life story is my testimony...

Unfortunately, I have to paint a vague picture of where my choices have taken me because I do not want to connect any missing information in any discoveries. My testimony begins and has similarities as most men of my age, who grew up in an urban area, single parent home without a father in the household but my testimony has a twist because of my active participation in church and because prayer has always been and is a constant in my life.

My father left when I was about 11 years old, but my grandfather was very active in my life until his untimely death. I was about 13 years old. As you know the teenage years are a transitional time in our life, it's a time when one experiences numerous changes physically, socially, and emotionally. Because my dad was gone and my grandfather had passed away I lacked positive male leadership, so in my quest to discover life, who I was, what I wanted to be in life I happen to rely and pay a lot of attention to what was going on, who had what, and who was doing what. I know there is nothing unusual about what I was doing because I was doing what teenagers do which is to explore and try to figure out my place in the world and even test the waters. My mom worked nights, so I had a lot of time to seek mentorship from my neighborhood friends and school classmates.

One day I asked this guy how he got everything he had, this dude had cars, clothes, jewelry and money. He told what he was doing to be able to have everything he had. What he told me was something that I was not willing to do and knew my mom would not go for it, so I promised myself that I would never do what my school mate was doing to make money. Note to self if you have *ever* been told to **never** use *never* please know that I am reminding you of this right now; Do not ever say what you will never do!

On more occasions than I wish, I have caught my mom crying about not being able to pay bills or not having enough money to provide for me, my brother and my little sister. It hurt me to see my mom crying, and as a male child I wanted to protect and provide for my mom so I made a decision based on emotions. So I went back to my schoolmate and asked him to teach me how to make money like him. One trip to the pawn shop I leave out with $120 and then I was on my way to being a Baller and got the nickname *Church Boy*.

I was making money enough money to be able to I hide money in my mom purse, in her dresser draw wherever so she could find it! I was making so much money from *"Petty Hustling"* as some would call it; but I was able to buy a car, a 1988 or 1990 Rally Sport Camaro that I had to hide 2 blocks away from my house. Every morning I would get up for school and proceed to walk like I was walking to the bus stop but I was walking to my car to drive to school. As with everything that you think you are getting away with, you eventually get exposed. A policeman who knew my mom and dad told my mom about my car; about what I was doing and that her house was about to get kicked in. My mom asked me and I told her that I wasn't. Yes, I lied to my mom because *I KNEW* that my mom would *NEVER* accept it!

Word to the wise if you have to lie to your mother, the one person who will have your back when everyone else is gone…that's an indicator that you should not be doing whatever you are doing.

After about 5 months of *"Petty Hustling"* I hooked up with my Aunt's boyfriend. He was a Bey of the Moorish Science Temple of America. With this connection, I took off! I took off so well that I started to need to buy more product than what he could supply me, as the familiar story goes "the Streets *ain't* got No love for you". My *Connect,* my Aunt boyfriend set me up to get robbed.

The robbery goes a lil something like this. I had the cash to buy 2 Kilo's, he counted the cash and wanted to leave with the money to go pick up the product. I told him to leave the money and I would give it to him when he came back with the product. He got pissed and said that the deal was off because I did not trust him and then he left. It was no secret that my mom worked nights, so when they came back around 11pm that night, they kicked in my mom's front door, tied me up and put me in a closet. From the closet they would ask me where the money, the money was gone. I tried to tell them that but they did not believe me. So, I remembered I had some money under something in the living room about $600. I told them where they could find the $600 they found it said that I had to have more money I told them I didn't because I did not, eventually they left. I waited about 2 minutes before coming out of the closet. I grabbed a gun, shot at them but I missed. I ran to my Auntie house and told her what had happened she calls the police, my uncle tell her not to call the Police but it was too late. So we made up a story to explain what had happened. However the police was not having it. They took me and my brother down to the police station and tried to question us. I was not charged because the crooked cops had something else in mind, they liked the Tech 9 I had, so they kept it and let me go. They let me go so they could watch me but at that time I just thought I had gotten away with something.

Word to the wise… you never get out of trouble easy. This was my first warning that should have caught my attention and my second warning came shortly after when my mom told me I could no longer live in her house. Two warning in one night should have been a wakeup call for me but it wasn't.

My girlfriend at that time was pregnant with our 1st child, so she and I moved into Springwood Apartments. Being out on my own increased my ambitions so I hustled harder so much that my friends and I needed another connect again, just by chance we ran into another buddy who had an out of town connect. This out of town connect required us to send our money out of town in a truck. I would fly to meet my money and Mexican Ike. Everything was going good until I started to notice some things that could lead to potential trouble. I was gaining a better awareness so I thought, but I had no vision of quitting even thought this out of town connection and the way it operated was filled with things that made me feel uneasy such as people someone running their mouth, being hot headed, showing off and trying to make it seem as if the operation was all of his masterwork. In the mist of my continued discontent, I would still get product from my local connect so either way I was good.

This is the mid 1990's and everyone was making money, moving product as planned so my local connect started to get more product than he could move. The brought the end to my highway journeys all together. I was moving like 200 keys a week, I was making so much money that I got scared or was it my inner voice from my upbringing in church speaking to? I got so scared that I quit and started walking around with a Bible in my back pocket asking God to forgive me. You see my spirituality had always playing a large role and has always been a constant in my life. So it was quite natural for my inner voice to speak to me in the mist of me living this double life.

A man cannot "walk the line" for too long…

As I said earlier, I was making so much money that of course I had to figure out what to do with the money, so I hid it in different people house. Once one person caught on of the possibility that I may have had stashed some money in their house folks started stealing my money. Looking back that was funny; people straight tore up the walls over all their houses looking for my money. The stealing of my money after a year of being out of the game, I led me back to hustling.

In this profession loyalty is close to not being in existence your family will steal from you and your best friends will set you up. My best friend from as long as I can remember turned into an enemy not once but twice. The first time we were about to go on a double date, but he kept saying he needed to meet someone, I was hesitant but we did it anyway. During the transaction, all of a sudden gun shots rang out, I ran out of the house and hid in the gangway the guy was looking for me but he was trying to get away so my life was saved. I went back into the house to check on my friend he was hit once. Once my friend healed he told me he was out of the game and I believed him. In reality my best friend was not being straight up with me, people tried to tell me that my best friend was still in the business of making fast money but by robbing and kidnapping people. Tupac said it best "your best friend will turn into your enemy" it was hard for me to believe that my best friend had become a robber, but it was even more difficult for to believe that he would rob Me! The curiosity led me to ask my best friend, he denied it and I believed him.

Time past by and as they say time reveals all things, and time revealed my best friends true intent, he kidnapped a mutual friend and drove him to Illinois and then he stopped the car, opened the trunk as he was opening the trunk our mutual friend yelled "*but I'm your friend*" that cry saved our friends life.

Two years pass by without me seeing my so-called Best Friend, but somehow he got my phone number called me and asked could we grab something to eat and talk. I agreed even though I did not trust him I went to get something to eat with him anyway. We went to Burger King, got us a meal before we could get back in the car he received a phone call, he confirmed where he was. Once we were back in the car, I noticed a man walking close to car, I asked for my friend to pull off but before he could another guy had slipped into the back seat of the car and pulled a gun out on us.

We were taken somewhere in Overland, MO and my so called *Best Friend* and I were separated from each other, but I was able to noticed that my best friend was talking to one of our kidnappers like he knew him. The guy who was guarding me at gun point asked me how long had I known my so called Best Friend I told him just about all my life, since I was about 5 years old, the kidnapper eyes showed a sign of disbelief. I told the kidnappers that I had some money in a car in a garage. They take me to the car, I was warned that I better not come out of that car with nothing else other that the money. I followed their orders, but they were not satisfied, they said I gave them the money too fast, so I must have more. I assured them that I did not. They left me and my so called Best Friend and said that we would find the car about 2 blocks from where we were.

I did not get into that car with my so called Best Friend, if I would have no telling if I would be here today to share my testimony. Youngsters stay true to who you are, to your family, your core values and do not enter into a life of destruction, greed, envy and jealousness.

My skilled talent enriches not only my life, but the lives of many others. Be a scholar! Be passionate about something! Pursuit knowledge and a lifestyle that gives life rather than a lifestyle that takes life away.

Let your Passion fuel your Testimony

Church Boy

P.S. "All young people believed they were immortal, and he had personal experience of the methods they used to cull themselves - base-jumping, sky-diving, hard drugs, alcohol. Over the years he'd come to see solid sense in the ways so-called savage peoples formalized their rituals of manhood; without such regulation, young men seemed compelled to invent their own, even more lethal, rites of passage."
— Alison Fell, *The Element -inth in Greek*

REFLECTION PAGE

"You are A MAN, not *just a man*; don't be diminished. Live up to your grand potential."   — Richelle E. Goodrich

CHAPTER TWENTY-SEVEN

To My Sons,

I remember when my father would take me with him to my Uncle Andrew's farm to hunt and fish. I'm sure my mother prodded him to do so. We would wake up in the bosom of dawn, his bones cracking and my eyes blurry, both of us yawning the night away. We would ride in silence mostly; my father was not a big talker. He was more of a grunter. He had the uncanny ability to answer almost any question with a "humph" and we would know exactly what that meant. When we got to my uncle's farm, we would immediately head to the small lake that bordered his property, digging in the moist soil for worms to bait our hooks. I would always try to catch a couple of fleet-footed crickets as a special delicatessen for the fish. I was convinced that if I found crickets, then I would definitely catch the most fish. My uncle would join us eventually, bringing coffee for himself and my father. I already had some type of juice in my He-Man thermos.

Although I look back on this memory, and most memories of my father, who passed away in 2003, with fondness, this was not always the case. When I was a little boy, I used to be embarrassed of my father. My best friend's father was a successful CEO and my other best friend's father worked for a trucking company. It was blue-collar work for sure, but he made pretty good money. Both of my best friends' mothers were teachers. My father, on the other hand, was a high school dropout, who worked in heating and cooling. They didn't really call it HVAC back then. My mother was a secretary at the time. Later in life, I found out that my father dropped out of high school and lied about his age so he could join the army and go fight in Vietnam. But as a young boy, I just thought that my father was a failure. I knew he was smart as a whip. He could answer any question you threw at him; he read constantly, he even would sit around the house and create new designs for air conditioning units. He and my mother would always preach to my sister and I that we had to go to college, but I thought they were being hypocrites because they never went to college themselves. At that age, I knew nothing of institutional racism and the lack of opportunities for African Americans.

At my father's funeral, my two best friends and I reminisced about my dad and it took me by surprise that they used to envy the relationship that my dad and I had. While I was busy being embarrassed by what my father didn't have and didn't accomplish, I was missing all the wonderful qualities he did have. It was my dad that taught us how to shoot a bow and arrow with a homemade target in the basement. It was my dad that made sure our Pinewood Derby cars were ready for competition. It was my dad that went to Dad and Lad camp. It was my dad that would get up at the crack of dawn to take his son fishing and hunting. Their fathers never did any of those things, always too busy or just never wanting to be bothered. While I was envying their fathers, they were envying mine!

Sons, I say all of that to say this. We never know where life will take us and whom life will bring into our lives. Remember to see people for who they are, not for what they can offer you. Take joy in the little things; it's in the little things that some of the biggest memories are made. Never look at another person's situation and lifestyle and envy what they have. Make the best life you possibly can for yourselves. You have the capacity to do whatever you want to do. Make your dreams a reality. Always remember, I'm here for you. Whatever you need, whether it's bear hug, a word of encouragement, or a couple of dollars to get you through the lean times, I will always here.

Love always,

Dad

P.S. go listen to *Dance with My Father* by Luther Vandross

REFLECTION PAGE

"Police are killing black men. Mona Scott-Young is killing black women."

— Darnell Lamont Walker

Chapter Twenty-Eight

Blessing Terry,

In hindsight there are so many things I wish I could share with *You*. In fact I have so many things to share with you that it would be too much to write in one letter. However, I will make an attempt to enlighten *Myself* to a few jewels.

One should never feel afraid to acquire knowledge. Although there will be times when *You* feel other things are more important, such as *Money*, but money will come and go; however education is *King* and it follows *You* wherever *You* go in the *World*, and it will prove to be useful *Your* entire life, even after the money is gone.

Life must have a balance and there truly are no shortcuts. We cannot be people who run from spirituality or religious beliefs. As humans, some of us naturally tend to share a common attribute of being a bit agnostic. But I feel that being agnostic is much better than being atheist. Because if *You* at least follow some form of religion, *You* will display *Integrity*, *Moral Values*, and *Humbleness*. Most beliefs teach us the practice of placing ourselves in someone else's shoes.

The fortitude and principles of a person means a lot in this world. If *You* do not stand for something, *You* most definitely will fall for anything. Life is too short not to *Value* other people's feelings, as well as just valuing the benediction of living as long as our natural life allows us.

Shortcuts may make us a lot of fast money; however it distorts our true value of *Love*, *Life*, and *Monetary Gain*. Not to mention ill-gotten gain can cause faster death as well as greater hindrance to one's physical freedom. *You* can attest to loosing far more than just time after incarceration. One cannot place monetary value over freedom. Nor should *You* feel that it's pusillanimous to work hard. Impecunious times will occur, but it is a far better feeling than little or no freedom. And trust *ME* losing *Your* freedom not only effects our life but it brings pain to all of our family members and friends.

As I come to closing this letter, one more thing comes to mind. As a man, desire to treat all women like queens. The main reason being, all human life as we know it comes through women. Our Mothers sacrificed a lot for us to not only have *Life*, but to instill *Integrity* as well as *Security* into us. *You* will find *No Love* as *Strong* as *Motherly Love.* If we take heed of such *Love* and the *Sound Advice* of a *Mother*, it will save us a *Lifetime* of pain and heartaches.

A letter to *Self* with lots of *Remorse* but no *Regrets* because the mistakes we make as well as *Our* greater accomplishments is what molds us.

One

Terry *"Southwest T"* Flenory

P.S listen to "Viva la Vida" by ColdPlay

Viva la Vida translates from Spanish into "long live life."

REFLECTION PAGE

"I don't stand for the **black man**'s side, I don't stand for the white man's side. I stand for God's side" – Bob Marley

Chapter Twenty-Nine

Dear Younger me,

First let me start by saying I'm very proud of you young man, amidst great storms and trials you've managed to succeed in life. I would also like to thank you for the decisions you made early on which allowed me to be who I am today. However, I would be remised if I didn't point out a few areas of concern, just some things that may help another young man out so he doesn't have to struggle like we did.

I'm just going to start when you were in the ninth grade; you were shell shocked completely thrown when you hit the hallways of University City High School. Dude you literally sat there a whole semester in the back of every class and did nothing but try to not be seen. My heart breaks for you just knowing how lonely that felt. Here's what you should've done. You should have talked to your guidance counselor, told him that you are scared and felt lost, that your parents, even though they loved you, they absolutely had no idea of how to help you with these emotions. You should have asked him for help, see your guidance counselor was a trained and educated professional who could have provided you with tips and ideas on how to break that mode, you could've excelled in school a lot earlier. See little Bro. It was absolutely normal for you to be afraid and not as responsive as some of your classmates, in fact many of them felt the same way they just hid it better than you. I would also like to thank you for not going with that sexually active twelfth grader, boy she was gone eat you alive (LMAO).

As you proceed in life be **confident** you are an amazing young man, learn not to need the seal of approval from others, allow your voice and feelings to be enough. Learn to embrace being alone, you're ok by yourself.

Embrace your fears and take them head on, let them motivate you to do great things. Don't let your failures keep you down get back up sooner and fight even harder. The same love and concern you give to others needs should be applied to you first.

There aren't many changes I would make with the decisions you made Sir, but one is your decision to get married at nineteen years old… Dude I cannot scream loud enough *"**Don't Do It**!* Read some literature keep your heart three stacks, keep your heart." No but for real, you were way too young for that, great attempt at manhood but this Sir that was an Epic failure… On the flip side **You** did learn a lot from that experience, some things that will carry you a long way with male – female relations.

Finally, I want you to know that you are only young once, live life and be free, challenge yourself, go places, take the scholarship to Alcorn University, don't worry about what you don't have and enjoy the things you do have. I love you and wish you the very best young man.

Peace

REFLECTION PAGE

"Racism is not an excuse to not do the best you can". - Arthur Ashe

CHAPTER THIRTY

This is How to Cheat Yo self…

Reginald Lamont Simmons; 37 years old, Date of Birth March 4, 1978.

Rap Sheet

Arrested February of 1996, released August of 1996. Arrested January 13th, 1997, released May 9th 1997. Arrested January 12th, 1998, released June 7th, 1998. Arrested November 19th, 1999, released April 6th, 2000. Arrested August 25th, 2003, Age 25, Released (Still Serving Time)…

See just the time it took you to read the above is the same amount of time it can take to make the wrong choice that could affect your life 4EVER…

What you have just read is a perfect example of being a statistic and recidivism. *Recidivism* is the tendency to relapse into a previous condition or mode of behavior. Recidivism is measured by acts that result in rearrests, reconviction or return to prison with or without a new sentence during a three-year period following release. I have to own the fact that my actions led to being me to mu current situation .

If you do not believe me read the research from the national statistics on recidivism:
- Within three years of release, about two-thirds (67.8 percent) of released prisoners were rearrested.
- Within five years of release, about three-quarters (76.6 percent) of released prisoners were rearrested.
- Of those prisoners who were rearrested, more than half (56.7 percent) were arrested by the end of the first year.
- Property offenders were the most likely to be rearrested, with 82.1 percent of released property offenders arrested for a new crime compared with 76.9 percent of drug offenders, 73.6 percent of public order offenders and 71.3 percent of violent offenders.

It has taken all of the above to happen in order for me to get it! Mass Incarceration is real! Don't let this be you too. This cycle of easily allowing the agenda of Mass Incarceration must come to an end; it has to **STOP** somewhere, so why not with you?

Please believe you do not want to cheat your family of time that you cannot get back and most importantly you do not want to cheat yo self. I do not want you to be a part of the reason why there is so many single mothers in the world; raising someone who you helped to create!

That's not being tha Man I know you are. Step Up and take care of responsibilities, be Loyal to yo woman the same way you were Loyal to yo friends in tha Streets.

Peace & Love
Reggie

P.S. Go listen to Jeezy a "Win is a Win"

REFLECTION PAGE

"If we accept and acquiesce in the face of discrimination, we accept the responsibility ourselves and allow those responsible to salve their conscience by believing that they have our acceptance and concurrence. We should, therefore, protest openly everything... that smacks of discrimination or slander". - Mary McLeod Bethune

CHAPTER THIRTY-ONE

THE GENIUS WITHIN
By Tony Morris ©

What is a genius? Some believe that a genius is a person with a high I.Q. or a genius is a person who knows what others do not know or understand about certain things.

I do not believe that the idea of who is a genius and who is not a genius can be determined by other people. I believe that it is determined by how each of us chooses to view ourselves and what we do in light of how we see ourselves.

I was a young man raised primarily in a single parent home by my mother. One of the greatest gifts that I have received from my mother was the love for reading. When I was a young boy and I wanted to know the answer to something my mother would either have me read a book or look it up in the encyclopedia. This was before the personal computer era. It would take me some time to find out certain things that I wanted to know about but once I understood those things I felt empowered and intelligent. She put me on the path to discovering my personal genius.

According to ancient Roman belief, a Genius was a "guardian spirit that was assigned to a person at birth." This guardian spirit was said to be personified through that person as a specific natural ability, a great mental capacity, an inventive ability, a quality, a disposition or an inclination. The dictionary backs this up by defining a genius as "a person with a peculiar, distinctive or identifying character."

A genius is simply someone who is in touch with who they really are as a person.

There is a popular movie that came out a few years ago that was based on a comic book series. It is called the X-Men. The idea behind the X-Men was that there was this man named Charles Xavier (or Professor X). Charles Xavier was the founder of a private school that trained people that society considered to be different than everyone else. They were called mutants. These people that he trained were not inferior to others rather they had superhuman abilities. One had to wear sunglasses because his eyes were as bright as the sun. Another had the ability to float in the air. Still another had the ability to produce storm like conditions whenever they began to spin around.

Many of these students that came to Professor X came to him angry and confused because of how others had treated them. They were different from the other young people that they had grown up around and had experienced treatment that made them feel less than human. Professor X helped each of these students recognize that their differences were what made them unique and what made them geniuses. They simply needed to identify their abilities and then harness those abilities for good. This is what each of us needs as well…someone to help us understand ourselves and what types of abilities, talents and gifts that we have in our lives.

When I look at the young men hanging out on the corners I think about the X-Men. When I visit the juvenile centers and see the young men and young women incarcerated, I think about the X-Men. When I visit the schools and see all of the students, I think about the X-Men. When I think about who will read this information, I think about the X-Men.

One of the greatest enemies you and I will ever face in our lives is the misconception of who we are ourselves. With a proper self-concept we can embrace all of ourselves including our pasts, and yet not limit ourselves to our pasts. We can learn self-responsibility, develop self-confidence and live our lives purposefully. This is what finding the **genius within** us all is about.

It may mean that some people will reject you along the way however, as long as you don't reject yourself you can realize the potential of that **genius within**.

We really have no idea what a person can achieve. The more we use and magnify our present talents, the more talents we will realize within ourselves. Just like the X-Men you have hidden abilities that no one has seen before. It is when you take the responsibility for being who you want to be that you will begin to recognize that you are as much a genius as anyone else.

Someone once said to me, "What you believe about yourself comes from where you get your information." I choose to get my information about myself from the creator and not from another person. Therefore, I will not have the limitations of other people's low expectations for me and I can raise my standards for who I want to be as high as I want them to be. You can do the same!

You are a **Genius** with an incredible mind and abilities. These abilities live within you and are simply waiting for you to call them to the forefront of your life. Now go and create the future that you believe is possible for you.

Unlock your Genius,

Tony Morris

P.S. Go listen to "Shining Star" by Earth, Wind and Fire

REFLECTION PAGE

"The question is not whether we can afford to invest in every child; it is whether we can afford not to". - Marian Wright Edelman

LETTER THIRTY-TWO

Dear Robert Lewis,

The first Robert Lewis, I would like to share some advice with is Robert Lewis at the age 11. Why the age 11, you may be wondering? At the age 11 things in our life start happening, we started to see and hear more which gave way for us to start recognizing and see things differently.

I have a few a short pieces of advice that I learned from out life Robert. The first piece of advice for you is for you to be very cautious about what you believe; *"believe none of what you hear and half of what you see"*. The second thing, I would like to share with you is for you to stay in school. School and learning is not always easy but stay in school to make yourself proud and of yourself! The next thing is coming to you third but it is actually the first thing you should always remember kinda like "the Golden Rule"… Mr. Lewis you should always respect everyone equally; men, women and children because what you put out there and how you treat people is defiantly what will come back to you. We… you are not better than anyone else in the world, regardless to what you have.

Young Robert there is going to be good people and bad people that you meet but remember to make your own judgements of people individually and accordingly and *NEVER* judge anyone before you get to know them. Lil Rob stay humble, patient, always let a people know how you feel, be upfront, always keep your word no matter what, be fast to hear and slow to speak, respect people space and feelings. Lastly, I'm telling the both of us that it is never too late to go back to school. Life has taught me that having an education will help us to survive in this world.

Love you,

Lil Rob

P.S. Go listen to

REFLECTION PAGE

"I can accept failure. Everyone fails at something. But I can't accept not trying". - Michael Jordan

LETTER THIRTY-THREE

Hello 18 year old Zachery Post, you do not know me per se, but I know you. This letter is for the purpose of helping you navigate through the next years of your life. First off, continue to be the positive, optimistic, funny, and hardworking guy that you are. Next, be careful who you trust outside of your core family and friends. But do not be afraid to have conversations with people of any form or fashion, because you can learn at least one thing from anyone in most cases, even a homeless person. Learn ways to be responsible with the money you make. Of course, still have fun but be sure to save some money each time you get paid, even if it is a small sum. I know you are not to focused on your credit or credit score right now, but be sure to always honor the obligations you have made with credit cards, car payments, etc. Always be seeking knowledge, and take heed to the examples that have been laid in front of you by other people's mistakes. Do not believe everything people tell you, do your own research.

I know it is hard living with your mother and all her rules, but try to stick it out as long as possible. Do not just go to college because people tell you that is what you're supposed to do next. Try getting a job first to pass time, and then develop a passion for something that you want to make into a career, and then apply for college. Remember, this is not a race. Go when you know you're ready. You have always been a creative guy. Go into a field that has something to do with design, since you love it already it will not feel like work. A college on the west coast will suit you perfectly. You have to get out of St. Louis in order to truly thrive. The career you choose must have a smooth transition into a great small business. Your entrepreneurial spirit is strong because you are destined to be a business owner. But keep in constant contact with your family and friends, they make you stronger. Keep the younger generation of your family in mind, because they will need the wisdom you learn passed down to them. Make your weaknesses your strengths, like mathematics and spelling. Try to read a book every month, because reading is actually really cool. Keep this in mind; Rich people have small TV's and big libraries, poor people have small libraries and big TV's. Have 100% confidence in yourself at all times, no matter what you are facing. Remember that no one is better than you, regardless of their status, knowledge, wealth, or race. Always demand respect, because your opinion does matter. Along with confidence, believe 100% that you can accomplish anything, I mean anything you focus on, it's in your DNA.

Okay, back to being a business owner. Remember that the #1 goal of any business is to make profits. Not just to say you own something. Continue to not be afraid to try new things, but know that people around you will not always support it. That's fine, they just don't understand. Still try them anyway! Be supportive to people stepping out and trying things. Support black businesses and culture. Ownership in the African American community is crucial for our growth as a culture. Read about the Jewish-American race, and apply those same tactics to yourself, your family, and your culture.

You must deepen your faith in God; he will always be there when no one else is. Also, it is important for you to abide by all laws. Be careful not to become victim to the justice system. Just because you went to a majority white high school, played football, wore American Eagle and Abercrombie & Fitch and was viewed as the "Cool Black Guy", that means absolutely nothing in the real world. Regardless of that, the police will view you as another young black criminal or thug whose life is worthless. Harsh reality I know, but you have to understand how not to get caught up. So do not brush things off like getting insurance on your car, or having current tags on your license plate. The police are looking for any and every reason to pull you over and get you into their system. Pay your tickets on time, every time. This will save you a lot of grief in the future …believe me. Read about the law, and always know what the police can legally do and not do. Stop and think about every decision you make, big or small. They all have consequences that can set you back a few years or propel you forward a few years.

Still enjoy life though. Meet women, date them and enjoy being a young man. At this age do not take any relationship too seriously, your young. Do not get caught up in the heat of the moment, have good safe fun! Then when you're around 23 or 24 find a smart, goal orientated, not overly materialistic, respectful, supportive woman to settle down with. She must love and respect your mother to the utmost and also her own mother as well. Let love develop, and do not force it. Make sure the woman you choose has her own goals, and support her in those goals. Also be sure that she will support you in your goals too. Try to be sure she loves you for you and not what she thinks you will be worth in the future. You will build a future together, so you must work together. Stay drama free, and don't' sweat the small stuff. Focus on the solution to your problems and not just the problem. Make moves in your life that will better you, and not hold you back. In a nutshell, listen, work hard, trust in God, have a plan, focus on that plan, learn, love, believe in yourself, offer help to those in need, but do not enable, and stay humble. Also it wouldn't hurt to be an early investor in Google, Under Armour, and LuLu Lemon, lol. No but really, if you follow the message in this letter, I am sure you will end up exactly where you want to be in life but sooner.

From Zachery Post at age 33 years old

REFLECTION PAGE

Sometimes you've got to let everything go—purge yourself... If you are unhappy with anything... whatever is bringing you down, get rid of it. Because you'll find that when you're free, your true creativity, your true self comes out. - Tina Turner

LETTER THIRTY-FOUR

Message to Young Black Men...

A wise man once told me that, "a player plays all games but master none". I never understood that statement as a Young Fool but as an older Wiser Man I can understand the power of that statement. As a young Black Man you must understand you are playing the game of life and it's truly a game. As in all games you have rules and competition.

As a Black Man my competitor is the European Man and the rules is knowledge. If I'm his competitor than you as a Young Black Man is his son's competitor for that spot in college or that job at that Fortune 500 Company. People will have you believe that this has everything to do race while some of that maybe true but most of it has to do with the alpha male mind-set to take and conquer. There were two rules of slavery that had severe consequences running and reading. Running because the slave master lost physical property and reading because he lost mental property. So as a young man you ask, what does this have to do with life today?

The United States is an education-based system without it you can't compete and everything that happens is by design to lessen you as a competitor. There's a reason why your school system is below average, why that gun was put into your neighborhood, and why the drug game was presented to you with such glamour. It's easy to fill an empty brain with foolishness but a brain full of knowledge can accept little foolishness. With an empty mind you are fed the subliminal message that your Black Woman is a Bitch, to be a Gangster and take that gun and kill your Neighbor.

Education will teach you that your Black Woman is a Queen and killing a Black Man is pure foolishness. Being able to read and being

Educated created and still create Great Men such as Frederick Douglass, W.E.B. Dubois, Malcolm X and Martin Luther King Jr. Leaders in competition; while foolishness creates Killers, Pimps, and Drug Dealers. So now I hope you can understand why they as in Slave Owners never wanted us as in Black Men to be able to read because being able to read meant that one, meaning us as Black Men could be able to have the fruit that can feed not only ourselves but future generations for a lifetime.

Young Black Man educate yourself, prepare for the competition, prepare for yourself, for future generations and for the competition. Set goals, achieve your goal, then set new goals and prosper as a Young Black Man.

The Future is yours,
Cornell Atkins
P.S. listen to Marvin Gaye Trouble Man

REFLECTION PAGE

"If you don't like something, change it. If you can't change it, change your attitude." – Maya Angelou

POEM 1

Don't Quit!   *Author Anonymous*

When things go wrong, as they sometimes will,
When the road you're trudging seems all up hill,
When the funds are low and the debts are high,
And you want to smile, but you have to sigh,
When care is pressing you down a bit,
Rest, if you must – but don't you quit.

Life is queer with its twists and turns,
As every one of us sometimes learns,
And many a failure turns about,
When he might have won had he stuck it out;
Don't give up, though the pace seems slow,
You might succeed with another blow.

Often the goal is nearer than
It seems to a faint and faltering man,
Often the struggler has given up,
When he might have captured the victor's cup.
And he learned too late, when the night slipped down,
How close he was to the golden crown.

Success is failure turned inside out –
The silver tint of the clouds of doubt –
And you never can tell how close you are,
It may be near when it seems so far;
So stick to the fight when you're hardest hit -
It's when things seem worst that you mustn't quit.

WRITE YOUR GOALS

"The secret to productive goal setting is in establishing clearly defined goals, writing them down and then focusing on them several times a day with words, pictures and emotions as if we've already achieved them." - Denis Waitley

1 YEAR GOALS

3 YEAR GOALS

5 YEAR GOALS

10 YEAR GOALS

LETTER OF THANKS

I reached out to men from all walks of life who contributed to make this book a reality. Some of the contributors I know personally and some only knew from Social Media or the contributor is a friend of a friend of mine. However, I asked men to write a letter to their younger self and give themselves some advice that was learned from living their life. The letters would be narrative and give a snapshot of their life story. I also asked for the letters to be reflective, inspiring and empowering needless to say a great cohort of men answered my request.

I am forever thankful to this cohort of men and fathers for being so willing to take a risk and share a part of their life to the entire world and for the entire world to judge. I am thankful to Letters of Empowerment to the Next Generation of Men and Fathers, Volume I Cohort for being risk takers, and for trusting me. I am grateful for this cohort of men because I know that the writing process and taking time to write may not have come easy for some, and *I THANK YOU*!

I would like for this cohort of men to know that our words are powerful! The letters that makeup this book are nothing short of being powerful testaments of everyday life, survival and realization written straight from the heart. Letters of Empowerment to the Next Generation of Men and Fathers, Volume I Cohort please be confident that your candid honesty, willingness to share our truth, hurts and endurance that we've held close to our heart will be lifesaving and healing for us as a community at-large. It is my belief the next generation of women, men, mothers and fathers will understand hardships and obstacles are a part of life. Obstacles will come to past, but how we respond and grow from the experiences that obstacles present is important and key to completing our life cycle.

In closing, we are in a historic moment of time and this book and our efforts to unite generations will last forever and for generations to come.

Once again thanks in advance to some and thanks *a **million*** x *a trillion*-x *infinity* to others.

Twyla E. Lee

P.S. "People who are crazy enough to think they can change the world, are the ones who do." – *Apple Computers*

ABOUT THE AUTHOR

Twyla Lee, Ed. S
Activist, Educator, Entrepreneur, Mentor and Mother
Saint Louis, Missouri

Twyla has one son who she loves dearly. She is also a loving daughter, sistah-friend and mentor who earned her Bachelor of Science degree in Secondary Education at Harris Stowe State College in Saint Louis, Missouri and she currently hold two masters degrees both in Education, one with emphasis in Curriculum and Technology Integration, the other focus is on School Administration and Leadership; She also hold an Education Specialist Degree in Administration and Technology Management.

Twyla started her professional career in Atlanta, Georgia as a high-school teacher in the Clayton County Public Schools in 2001. Throughout her teaching career she exemplified effective classroom instruction and management techniques and has been noted by administration for utilizing and demonstrating effective communication skills, mediating student conflicts, working well with at-risk learners, being a flexible team player, and possessing the ability to work professionally in culturally diverse groups. After 14 years of teaching Secondary Social Studies, coaching, and mentoring Twyla has begun a new chapter. She is teaching Education courses at a university in Saint Louis, Missouri.

Twyla's purpose and the heart of the Letters of Empowerment to the Next Generation of Men and Fathers book is to have a resource for our young men, and for our young men to have a resource of understanding and inspiration as they navigate through life events. Secondly, the intent of this book is to share insight from the male perspective in hopes of building us all up to be more united, secure, strong, and loving towards each other.

"There are two primary choices in life: to accept conditions as they exist, or accept the responsibility for changing them." – *Dr. Denis Waitley*

REFLECTION PAGE

Use this page to write a thank you note to the writer of the letter from this book that you most identified with. Please include the name of the writer or page number with each thankyou note! Send thank you notes to Bridge the Gap314 4579 Laclede Ave #122 St. Louis, MO 63108 bridgethegap314@gmail.com

Proceeds from the sales of this book will be distributed by Bridge the Gap314 501(c)(3) nonprofit organization to other nonprofit organizations that seek to fill gaps in education and provide social services to individuals.

Organizations that are interested in a partnering with Bridge the Gap314 please send inquiries to bridgethegap314@gmail.com

Purchase options:
Letters of Empowerment
to the Next Generation of Men & Fathers

Available from Amazon.com and other retail outlets; on Kindle and other devices.

Men.   **Mentoring.**   **Men.**

Made in the USA
San Bernardino, CA
04 March 2016